Dolly Parton

Melodies of a Legend

CONTENTS

CHAPTER 1

DOLLY PARTON EMBODIES THE WORKING WOMAN'S FIGHT

When Dolly Parton's Christmas of Many Colours, a film about crises and miracles in East Tennessee, appeared on television in November, wildfires were raging in the Great Smoky Mountains, where she first strummed a guitar. As the smoke cleared in Parton's hometown of Sevier County, the dead toll had risen to fourteen. Tennessee Governor Bill Haslam told the New York Times that it was the state's largest fire in a century.

Parton said hours before the film's premiere that her Dollywood Foundation would pay a thousand dollars each month for six months to any family who had lost their house. Around 900 families would apply for the cash.

When I announced Parton's fire-victim fund on social media that evening, a West Virginia acquaintance and filmmaker who studies Appalachian poverty replied, "My first words after the fires: Dolly will save 'em." As she typed this, 11.5 million people tuned in to witness Parton play a generous sex worker scorned by self-proclaimed Christians in her hometown in Christmas of Many Colours.

Much has been written about auburn-haired "Jolene," the real-life siren Parton claims worked at a bank and flirted with her husband when he came in for a business transaction; she inspired the most covers of her hundreds of original recorded songs. But the blond "town tramp" Parton loved as a child is the lady to whom music owes far more. Parton modelled her look after the woman.

"Yellow hair piled on top of her head, red lipstick, her eyes all painted up, and her clothes all tight and flashy," Parton recounted in a 2016 interview with Southern Living. "I thought she was the most beautiful thing I'd ever seen." When everyone commented, 'Oh, she's just garbage,' I thought to myself, 'That's what I'm going to be when I grow up!' Trash!'"

Parton, now 71, has repeated this story numerous times since her appearance leads people to demand an explanation. In "Christmas of Many Colors", she eventually gives full respect to the "painted lady" by making her the guardian angel of a story partially based on Parton's childhood Christmas.

In the film, a young Dolly sits on a sidewalk strumming a guitar on a frigid December night while holiday shoppers swarm around her tiny hometown's main street; she's trying to help her father and siblings come up with $69.95, plus tax, to finally get her mother a gold wedding band. In her tight clothes and high heels, the yellow-haired woman drops a twenty-dollar bill into Dolly's guitar case—but a self-righteous shopkeeper sweeping the pavement refuses to allow the joyful youngster keep money contaminated by the woman's misdeeds.

"You get away from her," chastises the enraged woman. "Why, this is a divine child." She doesn't want your filthy cash." She says, before sweeping her broom at the woman, "Comin' around decent folks all painted up, sticking out everywhere."

"Boy, you and that broom make a good team, you ol' witch," Parton's figure responds before clicking off into the darkness, apologising to young Dolly for not being able to give her the money.

This distinctive Parton trifecta—eyebrow-raising tight clothes, generosity of heart, and a no-nonsense attitude—is an underappreciated, unidentified type of feminism that I identify in the hard-luck woman who raised me. They didn't sell their bodies, but they were mocked for their origins. The majority of them dropped out in the ninth, tenth, and eleventh grades. In our lives, there was no feminist literature or theory. There was only life, and we were women who were economically disadvantaged, working on our feet in restaurants and industries, and sexualized horribly.

My mother's long red artificial fingernails didn't slow her down when she was driving a UPS truck in the 1980s, pulling and pushing boxes of Christmas presents she and her own family wouldn't receive. Her other job was doing makeup to middle-class ladies at a department store counter in a Wichita mall, where a male manager would pass by to fix the metal name tag pinned to her blouse. She was well aware of what was going on and neither enjoyed nor objected, the latter being perilous for a woman who needed to keep her job. She recognized that the only way a woman with no money or connections could beat the game—that is, pay her and her children's bills—was to play it.

Parton's exaltation of the strengths of this sometimes demonised class of American woman in her songwriting, film roles, and stage character is both the most self-aware gender performance in modern history and a genuine representation of who she is. She represents the impoverished woman, the working-class woman whose feminine sexuality is frequently a survival tool and whose rugged presence may be deemed "masculine" in parts of society where women haven't traditionally worked, where the archaic image of a "lady" clings. They are single mothers in need of assistance and abortions, ladies without diplomas but with strong ideas, and complex people who have been reduced to a "backwards" cliché in the media. They have few ambassadors to convey their grace because they have long been humiliated as a moral blight in the United States.

What Parton has done for feminism has less to do with feminism and more to do with Parton, who is synonymous with rural poverty. She came by it naturally, as my grandmother would say about what alchemized a future mythology in those Appalachian hills in the middle of the twentieth century.

OUTTA THAT HOLLER

Parton was born on a small farm in 1946, the fourth of twelve siblings; her father, Lee, paid the doctor a bag of grain for the delivery. Growing up in feed sack gowns didn't make her sad, but rather thankful, as many fans of her songs know—a trait that has helped her become a very affluent woman. Year after year, royalties flow in for her iconic 1971 ballad "Coat of Many Colours," about cherishing a robe her mother made from scraps despite being mocked at school.

Parton has stated that her dedication to her mother, Avie Lee, is her favourite of her many hits. She traces her musical ability to her father's family, whom she describes as "dreamers." During Parton's childhood, radios, record players, and electricity had not yet reached the rural poor, so they entertained themselves in their own homes with antiquated traditions passed down from European country peasantry. Her maternal grandpa, a Pentecostal priest, was a singer and fiddler.

Billy, Avie Lee's guitar-playing brother, spotted young Dolly's musical talent. He helped her get on Cas Walker's Farm and Home Hour, a Knoxville radio and television show. When Dolly was eight years old, Billy apparently gave her her first actual guitar, a child-sized acoustic Martin, to replace the one she'd fashioned from an old mandolin and two found strings. He helped her write her first song, "Puppy Love," when she was eleven and recorded it in 1959, when she was thirteen, after a thirty-hour bus ride with her grandmother to Goldband Records in Lake Charles, Louisiana.

Rock & roll, which had its origins in Southern Black culture, was sweeping white America at the time, adding country elements. The peppy dance beat of "Puppy Love" and Uncle Billy's suave Elvis-style pompadour both reflected this. Parton idolised rockabilly pioneer Rose Maddox, the daughter of Alabama sharecroppers. But it was Appalachia's old songs, the poor European relative to slavery's African blues, that first shaped her. In "Apple Jack," one of her early successes, which she has said is based on real people, she sings of visiting a mountain-music man who left her his banjo when he died—a bit of Africa that had made its way to East Tennessee over the years.

Parton credits her business skills to her father, a tenderhearted lifelong labourer who didn't learn to read or write but was competent in the horse trade and could stretch a little money a long way. Her father's high valuation of their low-income property influenced her astute business sense, which helped her build an empire worth hundreds of millions of dollars.

During her Pure and Simple tour in 2016, she described two seemingly opposing interests: "getting out" and "being where you most belong" onstage in Kansas City. The glamour and glamour of support bands and extravagant productions seen on many of Parton's tours were pared away, leaving her on a relatively barren stage with three backup musicians and a few cascades of white cloth. The event started with crickets and lamps that flashed like lightning bugs.

During the concert, Parton went a few stairs to sit on a white platform described as a front porch, but it turned out to be an elevated area for communing with heaven. Before singing "Smoky Mountain Memories," her 1978 ballad about poor labourers driven north during the midcentury industry boom, she paid thanks to her father's hard work, economic decisions, and commitment to his family.

"Lee, you should go up your hair, get those kids outta that holler," her father had been told. Lee, however, announced that he would die in the East Tennessee mountains after a brief stay in Detroit when Dolly was a youngster. He knew they wouldn't have much, but they'd have food and shelter—and they'd be home.

To begin the song, Parton stood up and played a flute. She couldn't sit during the performance because her father deserved a standing ovation, she explained. Thousands of people stood up in an instant— her crowds would do the Hokey Pokey if she asked—and Parton chuckled.

"Not from you!" she exclaimed, as the audience laughed along with her. They then sat and cried while she sang.

Turning to Avie Lee, Parton built up "Coat of Many Colours" with parallel stories of her mother's ingenuity in the face of adversity. Avie would send the kids outdoors to pick the best rock for her to prepare "stone soup" with, always meaning to choose and praise the child who had the roughest day, Parton recounted.

Parton, who told the audience her family had running water "if we ran and got it," must have gotten her humour and natural poetry from her mother's vocabulary. "If we had some ham, we'd have ham and eggs—if we had some eggs," Parton told the audience, quoting her mother.

Parton has told such stories for decades—after all, she spent eighteen years at her parents' cabin, compared to more than half a century in Nashville and beyond, the majority of which she spent at the pinnacle of fame and money. Fans who have heard it a thousand times willingly line up to hear it a thousand and one times, possibly because such experiences are so rare among entertainers. You can tell who owns anything by its sense of humour.

Women in poor areas are more likely to joke about poverty, whereas more fortunate people tend to regard it with profound sadness—a manifestation of their own sense of guilt, maybe, or a lack of understanding about what causes happiness. Firsthand experience allows for a more comprehensive story than a solemn lament. Those women never had to pretend to be pleased by things their husbands couldn't afford to buy, and there's a dry humour in the gap between one's reality and the middle-class pictures in magazine advertisements.

When my grandmother told me about my biological grandfather's proposal to her when she was sixteen and pregnant with my mother, she did so with a laugh and a cigarette draw.

"It wasn't anything like, 'Please be my beloved wife.' "Sheeeeit," she exclaimed, and we both laughed—not at our own family's tragedies, but at the delusions of ladies who received a romantic proposal and a large diamond before spending a lifetime pushing a vacuum.

You haven't heard much of Parton's work if you don't discover that edge. Her early songs' recurring themes include hypocritical, angry, and even deadly men; women being used, ignored, and shamed; and dying infants. (The infant sibling Parton was responsible for as a child became ill and died.) Parton is known for her "fake" appearance—wigs, synthetic materials clinging to a surgically changed physique, pink artificial nails—but when she writes, she can be a very grim reality. The divine feminine of American roots music is that darkness in a woman's voice, plain stories of hell on earth sung by women who have little to carry them forward but faith.

"Little Sparrow," from her 2001 album of the same name, combines bluegrass, folk, and country gospel sounds from her own country, and is sung in the voice of a jilted, saddened mother telling young girls to "never trust the hearts of men." Parton, who is known for undercutting solemn times with endearing nervous humour, introduces the song with a joke onstage: "I call it my little sad-ass song."

Parton claims that you can't come from her hometown and not enjoy sad songs. In her songwriting, the worst things she relates about those mountains seem to match what she observed outside her family's house. Her father's refusal to say "I love you" was a widespread cultural affliction for males of all classes at the time and, possibly to a lesser extent, still today. However, Parton believes that her home was so full of love that any material privation was offset.

At another stop on the same tour, in Austin, Texas, after the poignant tribute to her musical mother and hardworking father, Parton made her way down the steps of the "porch" before it was carried offstage.

"Time to come down from heaven, I reckon," she remarked, as a strong, bare-armed man in a black vest and hat previously described as her "sexy cowboy" performed a new instrument. (By this point, she'd mastered the guitar, dulcimer, and flute.) It was white and rhinestone-encrusted, like all of her other instruments, including a grand piano she used for one number.

"Oh, the cowboy brought me a banjo," replied Parton. She was soon shredding on it with her talon fingernails while singing "Rocky Top," a bluegrass tune about the Tennessee highlands. It was penned in 1967 by a married couple of innkeepers just up the road from Parton's hometown of Gatlinburg, Tennessee, which was the hardest devastated by the recent wildfires.

Parton swung the banjo over her back during the bridge, and the cowboy handed her a fiddle. Parton touched the air with her bow like a conductor as the quick beat pulsed and one of her bandmates played another banjo. She aimed the bow at the cowboy and said, in time with the music, "You dance." While she fiddled and the crowd screamed, the handsome cowboy hooked his thumbs into the belt loops of his tight pants and kicked up his heels.

Parton spends more time onstage than the normal performer, deferring to others with what appears to be genuine humility—praising the audience, thanking her own band, recognizing her family and roots. But it was Parton's own delight, desires, and power on display at that point in the act, tears still moist on faces after the painful songs for mama and daddy. She sang the song, played two instruments on it, and the hot guy next to her was on her payroll. When she said "dance," he did so.

Sex, along with music and religion, was the third formative pillar in Parton's life, she said in her 1994 autobiography, My Life and Other Unfinished Business. She used to stalk an abandoned church with broken windows and buckling flooring where teens left condom wrappers under the porch; inside was a defunct piano and "dirty drawings" on the walls when she was younger. Parton claimed that in that environment of music, sex, and God, she had a spiritual epiphany that "it was all right for me to be a sexual being." She has admitted to being hormonally precocious both on the inside and out.

Her form, while notoriously raised, nipped, and tucked over the years, was as implausible as it organically developed. The men' attention alerted her to her sexual power at an early age, and she embraced it, dyeing her lips with iodine from the family medicine cabinet in the absence of lipstick. In the viewpoint of her people's traditional patriarchal faith, her desire for seductive behaviour did not honour her father and mother.

She reported her father punished her for making herself up in a 2003 Rolling Stone interview. " 'This is my natural colour!' she had insisted. "The more Daddy rubbed it off, the redder it became." 'This red ass of yours after a whipping, is that your natural colour?' Oh, I've been getting a lot of whippin's over cosmetics."

Her mother and preacher grandfather both trembled, fearful that the devil had led Dolly down Jezebel's path. During her television show Dolly in London in 1983, Parton referred to herself as "the original punk rocker." As a girl in the early 1960s, she pierced her own ears to hang feathers from them and ratted her hair. When her mother indicated she'd been possessed, Dolly Parton reminded her to give credit where credit was due—not to Satan, but to herself.

"I couldn't get my hair big enough or 'yaller' enough, I couldn't get my skirt tight enough, I couldn't get my blouses low enough," she wrote in her memoirs. "... Of course, I needed to get away from home in order to really put on the dog." I'd go into the Woolworth's four-for-a-quarter picture booth, unbutton my blouse, push my headlights up with my arms, and take shots."

What women who didn't grow up on a farm may overlook is that in Parton's hometown, this frequent act of female adolescent disobedience wasn't only about enticing males. It was about asserting her femininity in a world where everyone, male and female, summoned "masculine" characteristics while downplaying "feminine" ones in order to survive.

"My sisters and I used to cling desperately to anything halfway feminine," Parton said in her memoir. "We could see pictures of the models in the newspapers that lined the walls of our house, as well as the occasional glance at a magazine." We desired to resemble them. They didn't appear to be forced to work in the fields. They didn't appear to need a spit wash in a dishpan."

Lipstick and store-bought clothing, for Parton, indicated not just a life outside of backbreaking labour, but also a level of economic agency that might shield a woman from attack. Indeed, studies show that impoverished women are more likely to be victims of serious male violence.

"Womanhood was a difficult thing to get a grip on in those hills, unless you were a man," Parton writes in her memoir. "[Glamorous women in magazines] didn't look as if men and boys could just put their hands on them whenever they wanted, with whatever degree of roughness they wanted." If a man wanted to touch them, he'd best be damned good to them, the way they looked."

Male violence affects women of all socioeconomic backgrounds. Parton's point of view, however, has a stark truth. She had white skin, good health, and a lot of talent on her side for the upcoming social rise. But everything that the world values less than a girl is a lousy one.

My family's poverty was tiny compared to Parton's, but it was enough for me to feel ashamed. We lived in rural Kansas, so I didn't notice it until I started school and saw other children's attire and lives to compare and contrast with my own.

That reckoning began before I even arrived at school on the first day: the bus rolled up to our long dirt driveway, and I stepped aboard with a paper shopping sack full of supplies. My mother had been checking off the teacher-provided list she carried in her purse with a little calculator and her plastic coupon organiser. But I was the only kid on the bus whose supplies weren't in a backpack, and by the time we arrived at school—nearly an hour after all the essential stops, snaking down dirt roads and ruts—I was ashamed to unload the new crayons and pencils I'd coveted from a paper sack.

If you're a quiet child, like me, who doesn't throw tantrums to express dissatisfaction, you have two options in such situations: drop your head and cry, or tilt your chin up and let the tears inside you convert into a salty form of strength. The ladies I knew had taught me the latter ability, which is especially important for a woman because she will be required to care for others as well as herself throughout her life. There is little room in such a life for one's own grievances.

Pain is transformed into force in all musical genres and, indeed, all kinds of creativity. For poor women, however, it is more than a song; it is a way of life, not just a performance. Parton's music, like that of Loretta Lynn, Tammy Wynette, Patsy Cline, and so many other female country musicians before and subsequently, reflects this.

TALKING THROUGH SONGS

Parton dedicated an area of images and mementos to Bill Owens at Dollywood, the theme park she founded in her home county in 1986. Parton sings a song to her uncle Billy from a small screen in a video recording seen by many of the park's 3 million annual visitors.

In the song, she remembers the two of them after chores were over thinking about a world far beyond those hills, and his instructions: how to select, how to yodel, how to shake her worries, and how to act in proper company. "You told me I was special," she says, "and I took it to heart." With the chorus, she repeatedly says "I love you," which her father couldn't say and Billy may have battled with as well.

Parton is currently the most successful female performer in country music history, thanks in part to that Tennessee man's caring guidance. She has sold over 100 million CDs and is a member of the Songwriters Hall of Fame; she has released over three thousand songs ranging from country to pop to bluegrass to gospel since 1964. She is one of six women to receive the Country Music Association's entertainer of the year award. Following the success of two blockbuster TV movies, a series recounting her childhood is apparently in the works.

Parton's forty-third solo album, Pure and Simple, debuted at number one on the Billboard country-album chart in August 2016—her first time in that position in a quarter-century.

Meanwhile, her work has received almost no radio airplay since the early 1990s, when Nashville's sound shifted dramatically away from twang. That didn't stop her supporters from cramming arenas in more than sixty locations during her greatest North American tour in twenty-five years.

When I surprised my grandma Betty with tickets to see that tour in Kansas City last summer, she had never been to a big-arena concert before, despite the fact that she and Parton were born eight months apart. As previously said, we are not a wealthy family with access to expensive theatre tickets. For the occasion, I had imagined us wearing similar shirts and pouring a can of Aqua Net onto matching beehives, but the trip and everything it represented to us—for one thing, I assume, that we weren't as destitute as we used to be—was overwhelming enough.

Betty and Dolly have somewhat similar origins, aside from being the same age. They each had an outhouse at home—Betty's was temporary, but it was still an extreme class signifier for her generation. They both despised school and felt like misfits. Betty, a fourteen-year-old waitress in Wichita, painted her hair green on St. Patrick's Day when she was fourteen; when the scandalised supervisor told her to go home, she refused to return rather than rinse the colour out of her hair. Betty was a really hot number in huge, blond wigs and miniskirts as a young woman in the 1960s and 1970s.

Betty fared slightly better in terms of resources than Dolly; her family had a car and a small house instead of a cabin, and there were four children rather than twelve. In the parenting department, she got a much worse hand than Dolly. Her father, a manufacturing worker raised on a farm west of Wichita, was a violent alcoholic; her mother, a restaurant cook and occasional factory worker, had untreated mental illness. That could be why Betty went on to live the life that Dolly supposedly only watched and documented in song: adolescent pregnancy, single motherhood, abusive husbands, adult poverty.

Betty used to put one of Dolly's tapes in the deck of her old car while we were driving down the interstate when I was a kid. In that emotionally restrained Midwestern culture and class, it's the only music I remember her singing and crying to.

Watching the concert in Kansas City with Grandma Betty, whose farmhouse I moved into permanently when I was eleven years old and who was only thirty-four when she learned she'd be my grandmother, was like watching two women's lives occupy the same space, with roughly similar beginnings but very different outcomes. I found myself observing Betty's reactions rather than experiencing my own—a habit that anyone from a troubled family may share, as observation becomes a way of both separating oneself in stressful circumstances and keeping an eye out for disaster. (People sometimes ask me how I remember so much from my childhood as a writer, and I imagine Parton's explanation is similar—if I wanted to live a different kind of life, I had to pay close attention to the decisions and situations of those around me.)

But I was mostly laughing during the concert.

"People ask me what it was like to work with Burt Reynolds," Parton added, implying that asking Reynolds what it was like to work with her would make a lot more sense. "Well, my best movie experiences were with women." The crowd erupted in delight when Steel Magnolias and 9 to 5 were mentioned.

After the final note of her new song "Outside Your Door," in which a lustful woman knocks somewhere she clearly shouldn't be, Parton said, "Open the dang door." You already know you want it." The audience laughed and cheered.

During a stillness a man screamed, "I LOVE YOU DOLLYYYYYY."

"I thought I told you to wait in the truck," she replied. Despite the fact that she's said that remark at every show since the Lyndon B. Johnson administration, the audience laughed and cheered.

She dismissed her drummer for being lippy, but that was fine because the piano had a drum machine on it, saving her thousands of dollars. The audience laughed and cheered once more.

"Jolene mighta worked at a bank," she explained before launching into the classic, "but I have been to the bank many times with this little song I wrote." On that one, the audience erupted in laughter and physically shook.

Betty laughed along the way, but not in the way she used to. Unlike Parton, she hasn't had high-priced physicians maintain her in tip-top shape throughout the years, and her knees were aching in our cramped seats halfway up the massive arena.

I got her to stand up and dance with me during "9 to 5," which had the entire audience on their feet near the end of the play, but a woman who lived the song might not be as happy.

Betty started as a clerk at the county courthouse in downtown Wichita in the 1970s, then became one of the city's first female police reserves officers and worked her way up to roles as a bailiff, subpoena officer, and probation officer for the criminal courts. She did it all as a woman who drew a lot of attention from men, including the same male attorneys who, in that work setting, would theoretically represent her in a sexual harassment complaint. It couldn't have been simple.

I was so concerned about Betty's enjoyment, even if it was only knowing she was craving a smoke, that it took me a long time to realise the performance was also a major issue for me. Though I grew up to be a die-hard fan of alt-country artists and spent years assisting my then-husband, a professional guitarist, load in and out of clubs, I had only been to one other mega-concert in my life. That was over thirty years ago, in the late 1980s, when my father—a carpenter for whom such a show was likewise a rare treat—surprised me by taking me to watch Reba McEntire perform at the Kansas State Fair.

Dad subsequently told me, with some sorrow, that he probably drank a couple beers and a whiskey before we left our gravel road and took the flat highway to the fairgrounds. McEntire was a sparkling, sparkly speck from where we sat in the bleachers when we arrived. But it was such a special time for us that Dad photographed the stage with our 110-mm film camera to verify we were there, while I sang along with every song.

After the show, product vendors were out of children's t-shirts, assuming they had any at all. So Dad waited in line to purchase me whatever they had left, which was almost certainly a wildly overpriced pink adult-sized T-shirt with a shattered heart and the title of one of McEntire's huge singles at the time, "What Am I Gonna Do About You."

Dad's car wouldn't start late at night when we exited from the busy parking lot. Headlights flashed by us till he started the engine with the assistance of a stranger. On the long voyage home through the dark country, I used my enormous new T-shirt as a blanket while sleeping close to Dad, and I wore it as a nightgown for the next two years.

My dad, a country boy, the youngest of six kids raised on a farm just down the road from the house he built us with his own hands, money for materials saved from a small concrete-pouring business he ran for a few years, never liked country music and went to the show for his daughter.

"How do you listen to that stuff?" he used to ask when my clock radio started playing 1980s pop-country first thing in the morning and I still needed to be coaxed out of bed to catch the school bus. "It's so sad."

Country music was primarily a female language in my home. It was how we communicated in a place where feelings were not discussed.

"Listen to the words," Mom would say, and the music on her record player, eight-track player, or tape deck would impart some lesson about life, men, or survival. Wynonna and Naomi Judd, K. T. Oslin, Janie Fricke, Lorrie Morgan, Anne Murray, and, of course, Dolly, Tammy, Patsy, and Loretta all contributed their voices. But the information was passed down to me from my mother since she was listening to those songs and I was there to hear them. Reba's hit "Little Rock"—about slipping a ring off one's finger, not a town in Arkansas—was on heavy rotation in our living room not long before my mother divorced my father.

One of my greatest pleasures is being able to trace my childhood against a soundtrack of assertive assertions sung by ladies in denim and big hair. We weren't a musical family, but the two women who raised me, my mother and grandmother, cared deeply about music that validated our stories—working-class girls, women, spouses, mothers—in ways that TV shows, movies, books, magazines, and newspapers virtually never did.

When the little prairie towns surrounding us were diminishing with economic ruin in the 1980s, living in the country meant frequent drives "to town" to buy this or that item or, say, to work at the Wichita mall for the holidays, as my mother occasionally did for extra cash. That resulted in a lot of highway time. Instead of chatting, Mom and I faced one other and sang the same words in unison— country music, usually performed by women, filling the voids of silence that rolled along flat Kansas landscapes. Mom's cigarette smoke streamed out her cracked window as she tapped the air with one of her long, red fingernails on the steering wheel.

"Letter Home," by the Forester Sisters, from their 1988 album Sincerely, is one of the songs we wore out on tape together and is about women indirectly connecting with each other. The lyrics are written in the voice of a twenty-nine-year-old woman writing to her mother to inform her that her husband has left her for another woman and the marriage has ended. My mother became a freshly divorced young woman a year after the single was released, albeit for different reasons.

"Letter Home" came on one day when I was an adult and sat in my mother's living room. We were ecstatic to discover that we had both recalled all of the words. I was a freshly divorced young woman at the time.

Mom went silent and listened to this stanza in particular, as if hearing it for the first time as a mother: "He said he felt like a man with her, and I watched them drive away / Children and rent—there was no time for tears, just time to carry on."

Mom spoke out, taken aback. "He felt like a man with her, and I watched them drive away'?" she blurted out. "How do you feel with this boot up your ass?"

We were doubled over with laughter. We didn't need to point out that every woman we knew, including ourselves, had only ever done the leaving, never the being left.

Mom stopped laughing as she got to the second verse about the women the narrator works with. "We raise our kids and our jeans still fit / and sometimes we go out at night," she said.

"Our jeans still fit," Mom replied gently, her gaze fixed on the horizon. "Yep." She nodded slowly, her smile gone, and one eyebrow raised in understanding.

What she did know was that a working-class woman's body type has a lot to do with her survival. Not because she wants to "catch a man"—the guys she's met are broke, too, and don't think she doesn't know it—but because the female form's significance as an object in society is one of the few abilities she possesses. Unlike pricey college degrees and high-status material items, her body is hers, and how she looks will influence her financial future: Whether she is attractive enough to work at the makeup counter. Whether the UPS manager, who is frowning because she is too little for the job, can be persuaded with a grin at the interview. Whether the risky loan will be approved by the banker.

(As it happens, Rush Limbaugh's talk show's periodic "feminist update," which often disparages women for their appearance, has utilised the Forester Sisters' 1991 tune "Men," which playfully presents a dismal picture of the male gender.)

The physical implications for the working-class woman extend beyond the sexual undertones to a plain matter of respect. Poor women are stereotyped in popular culture as being overweight, with terrible teeth, and wearing bad clothes. Every contact in a woman's day is influenced by her health and looks, both of which are class signifiers. Each of those exchanges determines the survival of the woman with no money in the bank.

Dolly Parton, of course, is one woman who understands this.

Parton's musical genius merits a discussion that goes much beyond gender and class. But the lyrics she composed will be forever linked to the body that sung them, and her fame will be long linked to having modelled her appearance after the "town trollop" of her native holler. She gained notoriety as a result of this; during interviews in the 1970s and 1980s, both Barbara Walters and Oprah Winfrey urged her to stand up so they could point out, without joking, that she looked like a tramp.

Johnny Cash was hailed for wearing black as a symbol of protest against the status quo and on behalf of the oppressed. But that's the difference between a man and a woman making a thoughtful fashion statement.

Women who lack a voice, a platform, or a college education are the ones who most fully comprehend what Parton has been up to for half a century. This, too, may be a source of affection between Parton and some segments of her audience—a secret that hundreds, if not thousands, of interviews have failed to reveal because writers and critics have failed to consider the question: What role has Dolly Parton's music, movie roles, and persona played in the lives of economically disenfranchised women used to being shamed or cast as victims?

There are several valid answers to that question, but one of them is as follows: Dolly Parton made a Christmas movie at the age of seventy in which a shooed-away sex worker returns at the end to save a little girl, and she casts herself in the part.

It's widely assumed that Parton never forgot her roots, that she never abandoned her community, the economy of which now revolves around her tourist attractions, the children of which receive books and scholarships from her foundation, and the recently incinerated homes of which will be rebuilt with her assistance. Less has been said about her refusal to abandon a certain stereotype of an American woman, the one whose trailer prompts the world to label her "trash." She isn't technically white, but she is unquestionably impoverished, and she most emphatically did not have the opportunity to study feminist theory in a college classroom.

Parton might have classed herself up decades ago by wearing less makeup, as ladies with money are accustomed to doing, or singing something that doesn't belong on the Cracker Barrel CD rack. Instead, she created her image and penned her songs in such a way that she can't sing or look in the mirror without representing women who go unheard and unvalidated on a daily basis. Parton's chat with the women is captured in the music. They're someplace wiping down mirrors in truck-stop diner restrooms while listening to country music.

THE GREAT UNIFIER

I was going through Twitter one evening last June, before Grandma Betty and I saw Parton on tour, and Parton kept showing on my feed. It was two days after the United Kingdom decided to leave the European Union, causing cultural and economic ripples around the world. "Is 'Brexit' the Precursor to a Donald Trump Presidency?" asked one New York Times headline. (By the way, the column answered the question incorrectly.) A gunman had slain 49 people in a gay nightclub in Orlando, Florida, just a few weeks before. Democrats had just stormed the House floor in Washington, DC, to hold a sit-in in support of gun-control legislation.

But, in the midst of the gloomy political tweet cloud on my computer screen, Parton emerged, clutching a little bedazzled saxophone. A few tweets later, she was back, this time in a video performing a cappella 1960s protest songs with her small band. Parton again! Political tweet, political tweet! I saw that some of my New York City pals were at her Queens event.

She'd just started the Pure and Simple tour, which I had no idea was going on. What were a slew of New Yorkers doing knowing more about Dolly than I did?

The Dolly tweets coming in from New York contacts were from a diverse range that included people of all races, ethnicities, religions, and sexual orientations. They were, however, all women.

"That majestic bitch just started playing a goddamn PANFLUTE [sic]," a person said on Twitter.

"Dolly Parton, sitting in a pew onstage, just got a stadium full of Nyers to shout 'Amen,'" another woman said. Then it occurred to me: "Nothing says #Pride like a stadium full of gays singing 'Here You Come Again' with Dolly Parton."

Suddenly, two New York acquaintances I had no idea knew each other were tweeting a conversation.

"Her voice is perfect."

"Dolly for life!" "I had no idea she was such a storyteller."

"About to fling myself at the stage."

I was amused, touched, and a little astonished at the time, having not yet been among Parton's live crowds. I've been chastised so many times over country music that, when I lived in New York for a few years, I threw a party with the sole intention of teaching people how to line dance and sending them home with CD mixes of something other than hipster-approved David Allen Coe. I think I assumed Dolly Parton would be adored only in certain circles.

Of course, I knew Parton was a global phenomenon, but I had underestimated the extent to which people who aren't "country" admire her—not just as a "crossover" musician, but as the down-home, almost religious demeanour she exhibited on her recent tour. Perhaps the most astonishing aspect of her unwavering focus on stories of poverty and rural life, sung from beneath a wig and rhinestones, is how much she is universally adored for it by individuals from backgrounds that couldn't be more dissimilar to her own.

My affinity for Parton and her songs as a fellow working-class woman from the country is only one aspect of her allure. Plenty of celebrities have large fans, but Parton's work and persona build a bond among seemingly improbable friends.

During last year's tour, Dolly drag queens turned and ordered entire parts of the crowd to sway to the music. Those who swayed appeared to include wrinkled people wearing Wrangler jeans, pierced teenagers wearing all black, big men wearing T-shirts that read "proud redneck," gay men who knew the words to every song, children who knew the same words, lesbian couples holding hands, college kids holding a beer in both hands, and most everything in between.

Being among them allows one to witness and feel the power of a woman who actually lives Jesus' teachings—love all, judge none—in contrast to the phoney Christianity that so much of Nashville's country music industry falsely espouses. It is an unfalsifiable energy. Everyone in the room senses it, and Parton expresses it bluntly.

"Wouldn't it be nice if we could take a little vial of this love energy out there?" she asked the Austin audience in December last year. People clapped and sobbed at the close of a difficult year in America, just before the start of another.

Parton nearly typically avoids politics, but her approach to the presidential election drew flak from both sides of the aisle last year. When asked what she felt about a woman running for president by the New York Times, Parton answered warmly.

"Hillary [Clinton] might make as good a president as anybody ever has," she told the crowd. "... I believe a woman would do an excellent job." Hillary, in my opinion, is extremely qualified. So if she gets it, I'll be there to support her."

Her conservative fan base screamed in the blogosphere and on social media, vowing never to buy her recordings or concert tickets again. Parton later clarified that "if she gets it" referred to the presidency, not the Democratic candidacy, which was not yet finalised.

"My comment about supporting a woman in the White House was taken out of context," the statement went on to say. She hadn't endorsed either candidate, she stated, later claiming in interviews that she hadn't even chosen.

The left screamed at the prospect of her voting for Donald Trump, who was the Republican nominee at the time. They, too, would never buy her recordings or tickets to her concerts again.

Of course, the vast majority will continue to buy. Parton is a terrific unifier not only beyond identity and cultural divisions, but also across today's severe political divide.

Patron infused her characteristic puns and self-deprecating quips into her 2016 concert tour, saying that whether Clinton or Trump won, the country will suffer from "PMS"—"presidential mood swings." She avoids politics, but if she did run, she'd have the hair for it—"it's huuuuuge," she added, imitating Trump. Perhaps they didn't need any more "boobs" in the race.

Such crowd-pleasing diplomacy may have something to do with business, but Parton has put her sales at risk numerous times in the same political climate that saw the Dixie Chicks ostracised by Nashville and country radio when they denounced then-President George W. Bush following the 2003 invasion of Iraq.

After decades of strong support for the LGBTQ community, she penned "Travelin' Thru," a song for the Transamerica soundtrack, in 2006. The song, which she sang as a best-song nominee at the Academy Awards, references roots music about difficult, transformational travels, such as the nineteenth-century folk song "Wayfaring Stranger" and the early twentieth-century country gospel classic "I Am a Pilgrim." That history is woven into the musical song, which commemorates the personal, public, and political difficulties of those shifting genders. Parton sings with a raspy raspy voice, "We've all been crucified, and they nailed Jesus to the tree / And when I'm born again, you're gonna see a change in me."

Parton reportedly got death threats as a result of her involvement in the film. But, as a cisgender, straight woman whose appearance is regarded weird and whose sex life has been pushed, she empathises with individuals who are demonised or branded "freaks" for their sexuality or gender experience. For years, rumours have circulated about her lesbian relationship with a childhood friend who is frequently by her side. She claims she would come out proudly if that were the case; she has been married to the same man for fifty years, a Tennessean who worked in the concrete business. She claims that her LGBTQ fans are drawn to her nonjudgmental acceptance of their sexuality rather than her own.

Parton's aversion to overt political discourse could be attributed to her upbringing. Many members of my family dislike discussing politics, not because they don't care, but because they lack the trained language or the time to engage with the chattering elite.

Even though I am a professional communicator with three college degrees, I have been chastised on Twitter for using the incorrect word or phrase. My point of view wasn't systemic enough, or my phrase wasn't widely used in intellectual jargon. Imagine you hadn't been to school since you were a teenager in a rural place before the internet, like Parton and the women in my family. I don't care how worldly you become; if that's your background, a conversation dominated by formal, scholarly voices will likely be scary or at the very least unsettling. Parton says in her 2009 graduating speech at the University of Tennessee that, despite all the stages she has commanded, she is frightened standing in front of an auditorium full of people in caps and gowns. Her voice shakes as she says it, which is unusual for a lady whose tremendous confidence has been publicly displayed for decades.

Whatever Parton's motivations for telling personal stories rather than polemics, it couldn't come at a better time in a globe riven with strife. Several of my friends—white, Black, and Latina, from all socioeconomic backgrounds—commented in the weeks leading up to the 2016 presidential election that Parton was a spiritual leader when political leaders failed.

Her politics, like those of any transcendent storyteller, occur at the human level, analysed as experience rather than abstract conceptions, and lived directly rather than tossed about in academic jargon. There is a place for both the self-contained story and the didactic argument. Parton specialises in the former.

Last year, she made a statement about race and immigration through her philanthropic pledge to reach every victim of the Tennessee wildfires, rather than through a political tweet. According to Dollywood Foundation executive director Jeff Conyers, the organisation was concerned that undocumented immigrants would forego seeking assistance. As a result, the foundation went out to Hispanic community leaders to emphasise, across language barriers, that they were not "out to catch" anyone. There were no queries or records kept concerning race, ethnicity, or citizenship when connecting people with relief assistance. Similarly, recipients were not obligated to provide reports or follow-ups, and they were free to spend the assistance money anyway they saw fit.

I recall my West Virginia acquaintance saying after the wildfires, "Dolly will save 'em."

One reason she can do so, it appears, is that a lifetime of projecting love while avoiding theology drives others to do good. Last December, she and her foundation hosted a traditional telethon, which was also live streamed online, to raise funds for fire victims. They made $9 million in a matter of hours. When Parton phoned, everyone from pop veteran Cyndi Lauper to young country singer

Chris Stapleton stepped up. While Parton was speaking with Billy Ray Cyrus, Paul Simon called in with a $100,000 commitment.

Parton has pals all throughout the world. As I was penning this tale in a Wichita coffee shop, a homeless man approached me and inquired what I was writing about. When I told him, he brightened up and regaled me with Parton's life story, concluding with praise for her voice's honesty in an era of digitally modified music.

"She doesn't need any of that," he explained. "No matter how many years pass and no matter what she looks like, her pipes are her pipes."

Perhaps it's no surprise that Parton's popularity seemed to rise in the same year that America appeared to be in decline. A broken creature seeks wholeness, and Dolly Parton provides it—one lady who embodies past and present, rich and poor, feminine and masculine, Jezebel and Holy Mother, the adventure of getting out and the joyful homecoming home.

"This is just everything," said one of my New York City friends who was live-tweeting from Parton's gig last June.

THE LAST LAUGH

Parton joked that she had to grow affluent in order to sing like she was poor again.

She was the same soul inside a bright poor child in that holler in the middle of the twentieth century. She had a loving family, a guitar, and an uncle as a tutor, and she yearned to go somewhere she would be seen. Parton has stated that she was the focus of nasty gossip in high school—rumours about what kind of girl she was. She couldn't go before she turned eighteen because she assumed her father would send a posse after her.

When she graduated from Sevier County High School in 1964, she was the first person in her family to receive a diploma, and each member of the class was asked to stand and express their ambitions.

She told her classmates in her University of Tennessee graduating speech that she was headed to Nashville to become a star. They erupted in laughter.

She kissed her family farewell and proceeded to the bus station the next day.

Her life, and the world, were on the verge of major change as she waited for the bus. The Civil Rights Act would be passed into law within a few weeks. The largest women's movement since the fight for suffrage was building. But Parton's experience in East Tennessee would serve as a basis for her songs, a roadmap for dealing with Nashville's men in suits, and a call to share prosperity with those in need.

Parton had no idea. All she knew was that she was heading to a big, new area to pursue something she'd been working on for years. She carried everything she possessed in her hands. Somewhere deeper, she held a belief that she was more valuable than the world had implied, as well as a sense of humour about what she had endured along the road.

"I boarded a Greyhound bus with my dreams, my old guitar, the songs I had written," she wrote in her memoirs, setting up a joke she has recounted many times, "and the rest of my belongings in a set of matching luggage—three paper bags from the same grocery store."

CHAPTER 2

DOLLY PARTON MASTERS THE ART OF LEAVING

Billboard magazine interviewed Dolly Parton about feminism in 2014. "Are you familiar with Sheryl Sandberg's book Lean In?" said the interviewer.

"What is it?" Parton inquired.

"Lean In—it is a book," the interviewer explained. "Have you ever 'leaned in'?"

"I've leaned over," Parton replied, laughing at a possible allusion. "I've taken a step forward. "I'm not sure what 'leaned in' means."

The fact that a legendary female trailblazer in music, business, and popular culture was not included in the current feminist discourse may reflect Parton's origins: a location where a woman's strength and independence are more about walk than talk. That talk—the articulation, analysis, and theory of progress toward gender parity—has been critical to social progress in the women's movement. What poor and working-class women do for the cause is equally important but receives less attention.

Their realities frequently resist the container of politicised vocabulary, which is typically the domain of college-educated individuals. However, "uneducated" women have witnessed the most painful consequences of gender inequality: impoverished mothers with hungry children, beaten wives who are too poor and rural to access the legal system, and work that is not only undervalued and underpaid but also causes the fingers to bleed. For these women, the struggle to survive is a declaration of equality that could be described as "feminist." But here's the catch: In my experience, they don't care what you label it, correct or wrong.

The Women's March and subsequent walkout on International Women's Day earlier this year showed the classic class chasm that runs through all political movements. With a confirmed sexual predator now in the Oval Office, today's critical political resistance owes much to the hard labour and rage of civically engaged women. However, who is able to participate in such activity is heavily influenced by economic agency. You can bet that the majority of photographs of protesters wearing pink "pussy" hats show middle- or upper-class women who can take time off work, get transportation to a protest venue, or afford a babysitter.

For a woman like me, a feminist who grew up in a place that resembled Dolly Parton's childhood home in rural Tennessee rather than a well-connected progressive hub, marches and strikes are something to celebrate while also being sceptical of. I'm glad to call myself a feminist, but I'm not satisfied with my context for the term—a privilege of education and culture that most women in my community do not have.

Working-class women may not be fighting for a cause with words, time, or money they don't have, but they have unparalleled knowledge of how gender works in the world. Consider the concept of intersectionality. A working-class woman of colour may not recognize the term, but she understands how her race, gender, and economic issues intersect better than anybody else.

There is intellectual knowledge, which is the stuff of research papers and think pieces, and experienced knowledge. Both are essential, and women of various backgrounds may have both. However, we rarely extol knowledge, which is the only sort of feminism that many working women have.

Parton's career took off at the same time as the women's liberation movement, offering a telling contrast between feminism as a political notion and feminism as it is manifested in reality. Parton, like most poor women, knew little of the former but excelled at the latter.

You won't get far as a poor woman unless you believe you are equal to men. That belief is unlikely to result in a "leaning in," Sandberg's probably sensible suggestion to middle- and upper-class women looking to grab the riches enjoyed by men in their professions and households. A poor woman's best option is frequently to turn around and walk away from a hopelessly patriarchal situation she cannot possibly alter with her minimal cultural capital.

It was 1964, a presidential election year, and the country was ripped apart by political unrest and tragedy when Parton left Sevier County, Tennessee. Young men were returning in caskets from Vietnam, and President John F. Kennedy had been slain less than a year before.

Parton recalls hearing the news of Kennedy's death over her boyfriend's vehicle radio while en route to play on the Cas Walker radio show during a school break in her 1994 autobiography, Dolly: My Life and Other Unfinished Business.

"I had loved John Kennedy... in the way one idealist recognizes another and loves him for that place within themselves that they share," she said in an email. "I didn't know a lot about politics, but I knew that a lot of things were wrong and unjust and that Kennedy wanted to change them." Her lover, on the other hand, reacted to the news by calling Kennedy a "nigger-lovin' son of a bitch." She quickly dumped him.

"I couldn't believe that a young person with whom I had shared intimacy and laughter could be so ignorant, biassed, and insensitive," she said.

The 1960s and 1970s women's freedom movement had not yet reached a fever pitch. Kennedy established a commission on women's issues, but the National Organization for Women did not yet exist. Females of all social strata were still confined as wives, mothers, and second-class citizens by strict, conformist gender stereotypes.

Some of that movement's core writings were yet to be published when Parton stepped off the bus in Nashville, but they would not have reached Parton anyhow. The women of her generation were too preoccupied with feeding hungry mouths, and some were even farther removed from conversation in a pre-internet, rural setting, to read such literature—written in a kind of English they didn't understand anyway. Parton's ability to learn to read was a gift from her father, a farmer and occasional coal miner who was illiterate due to a lack of schooling.

Parton, on the other hand, was living feminism without knowing about it. Leaving home alone, as a woman with professional ambitions but no financial means, proved that she desired and believed she deserved a better life, even though no model existed for the trip ahead beyond her own imagination.

Meanwhile, the place she'd pursue that life—the country music recording capital—couldn't have been a more terrifying gauntlet for a woman. Even if America had a few little gaps in the roof that kept women down by then, Nashville was squarely under the thickest glass.

Patsy Cline, who died in a plane crash the year before Parton arrived in town, had lately challenged the industry's old-boy network, in which women were nearly never the main attraction. She ventured to wear pants onstage at the Grand Ole Opry in 1960 and was called over by a male emcee to be disciplined in front of the audience. That was the kind of heat tenacious Cline was born to take and throw back, but she couldn't overcome economic injustice while leading the way for women. According to the PBS documentary American Masters: Patsy Cline, her first record contract in the 1950s paid her half what males were paid and reserved all publishing rights for her label. This shackled her voice to the demands of the studio. Cline, desperate to leave her own low, working-class roots in Virginia, preferred it to her former job cutting chicken throats on an assembly line.

It was a difficult road for a female singer-songwriter, and Parton's ambitions did not come true as swiftly as she had planned. She was soon so poor that she had to feed herself by stealing food from grocery shops or wandering hotel corridors in search of room-service trays left outside doors for pickup.

She developed a tiny name for herself around town performing mercenary work: live spots on early-morning radio shows, a jukebox conference in Chicago. She rose to prominence as the uncredited background singer on "Put It Off Until Tomorrow," a successful pop song she co-wrote with her uncle and was nominated BMI Song of the Year. The following year, 1967, Parton was given the opportunity to record her debut country song, "Dumb Blonde." It went on to become a Top 10 smash.

The irony of Parton's big break being a song named "Dumb Blonde"—an admonishment of a man who calls a woman stupid. Its motif, a woman being smarter than the male who underestimates her, will recur throughout her career. Parton didn't create the song, nor did she write most of her subsequent songs, but she lived it so thoroughly that she couldn't even sing it on television without a man doing the same thing the song expresses.

Parton, 21, wore a fitted orange dress with a high neckline to perform her classic number on the syndicated The Bobby Lord Show. Her big blond beehive was a couple inches higher than the mainstream average, but there was no sign of country or the over-the-top appearance for which she's become famous.

However, when Parton spoke, her East Tennessee accent came through, as did the fact that she was more capable than the male host. Someone had planned a silly segue to her performance in which Lord intended to call her a dumb blonde with a well-timed pause—as in, "Why don't you go sing, dumb blonde," rather than "Why don't you go sing 'Dumb Blonde.' " Parton did her part—smile and seem confused—but Lord couldn't deliver the phrase correctly on the second try, and the joke fell flat.

Nonetheless, enduring such humiliations in exchange for exposure or a tiny payment proved to be a wise investment. Porter Wagoner, whose country music hour was the number one nationally syndicated show on television, told Parton in her autobiography that he had been watching her work and spotted "something magical" in her. Will she appear on his show? The salary offer was $60,000.00.

It was a rip-off given Wagoner and the show's affluence, but in Parton's eyes, it was a fortune. Of course, she said yes.

Parton's huge bet—leaving home as a girl with only two dimes to rub together at a time when her own mother was already married with two children in a Smoky Mountain holler—had paid off. But she'd gotten herself into another bind: a protracted, often excruciating stint on The Porter Wagoner Show beside the male host's booming ego. But Parton will never again stalk hotel corridors looking for remnants of room-service meals.

Parton purchased her first new car with that first sum of money, according to a 2014 interview with Billboard. She was married at the time to a man who operated a concrete-pouring company, and his preferences dictated the type of car she would have.

"I think it was a Chevrolet," Parton went on to say, "because Carl, at that time, only drove Chevrolets."

She, like many other women, especially poor ladies, didn't know how to drive. She crashed the blue station wagon into the wall of Nashville's Studio A on her way to record with Wagoner for the first time. It's poetic that she rolled up and knocked bricks off a powerful recording studio in the man's world where she was tearing down walls. The bricks were replaced, but they were never quite the same.

"When [the studio] used to do tours," she explained to Billboard, "they'd go around and say, 'This is where Dolly Parton ran into the wall."

HAVING ENOUGH

The majority of poor women's chances do not result in fame and money. However, the lives of the women I grew up with—aeroplane-factory workers, cafeteria cooks, discount-store cashiers, diner waiters, and fast-food workers—all share a common thread of drastic, self-preserving departures. The stories they told me about their lives in the past and present could be summed up in one phrase: "I had enough of his shit."

In the story, "he" may be an abusive husband, a dishonest partner, or a harsh boss. The little Colorado town that rejected my then-twenty-something grandmother for wearing mini-skirts and not behaving "properly" in the 1960s, or the Kansas village where her teenage sister was chastised for being pregnant out of wedlock, were both hostile places. For them, leaving was not so much a hopeful act as it was a necessity for existence, either physically or psychologically. Because of my family's situation, the next man or place was frequently no better than the last. They could, however, depart again, and they did. My grandmother Betty had divorced six men before the age of thirty-two.

The first one fired a gun at her. The second abducted her son. The third one shattered her jaw. The fourth was a temporary business partnership in which she could demonstrate to the courts that she had a spouse, as an attorney had required during her attempts to reclaim her kid, and he, a Mexican immigrant, could obtain a US visa. The fifth turned out to be emotionally traumatised indefinitely by his stint in Vietnam. The sixth one was verbally abusive to Betty and my mother, who was a teenager at the time.

"It wasn't gonna get it," my grandmother would say about every unpleasant circumstance she left behind.

The majority of that relationship drifting occurred prior to the peak of second-wave feminism, which Betty was unaware of. She was unaware of the patriarchal background of the institution of marriage, which future middle-class ladies would learn in women's studies classes and discuss at meetings. She had never heard the term "patriarchy" before (neither did I till I was a young woman in college). She only knew she wouldn't let a man, town, or boss treat her or her children badly.

Jobs and locales proved to be as fleeting as romance throughout those years. Betty worked countless jobs and journeyed across the country with my mother, great-grandmother, and aunts in quest of a better home, smoke shooting out of a rattling jalopy's window, cigarette in hand that no longer wore a ring.

One could be tempted to believe that a woman with such a résumé can't remain put, that it's her nature, rather than her circumstances, that drives her to seek trouble and flee again and again. Perhaps her lack of self-esteem pushed her into such heinous scenarios. But that would be underestimating the number of harsh hands a young lady in poverty may be dealt in a row in the 1960s.

Betty kept her cards when she finally acquired a couple of excellent hands. When a job-training grant for women helped her obtain a job as a secretary in the Kansas courts system in downtown Wichita at the age of thirty, she became a state employee and stayed one for decades until her retirement. Soon after, she married the guy I grew up knowing as my grandfather—a fun, loving farmer who was the first man in her life to treat her right—and lived on his farm for the next twenty-two years, until his death.

A middle-class woman may fight for gender equality in her corporate office and insist that her husband change diapers and vacuum; she may organise political meetings and write letters to local newspaper editors demanding that her daughter's basketball team receive equal coverage as her son's; she may donate money to Planned Parenthood and use some of her hard-earned savings to march with other women in Washington, D.C. All of these excellent efforts entail utilising some existing sliver of agency within an organisation to effect change. That middle-class woman is trying to improve women's roles in the workplace, the home, public policy, and politics. Those realms have become welcoming enough to her that she may stay and change them.

The poor woman has far less social, economic, and cultural capital to change things from the inside. But she might have a car and some petrol money, which is enough to get her out of a bad position.

Regardless of one's financial situation, there is a strong wisdom in simply leaving the nonsense for someone else to fix. When I was a professor at a tiny university with a strange history of tenured female academics departing, I realised this. Even middle-class women, those of us who have the ability to stay and strive to change the environments in which we find ourselves, recognize that we could give our entire lives to shift things an inch. Is an inch really worth our lives? I quit five months after being appointed.

Several of my middle-class female pals thought I'd gone insane. I had no financial stability or prospects outside of that employment at the time. I did have a mortgage and a significant amount of student debt. But my position at that university featured a daily grind of misogyny not dissimilar to the slaps on the ass I'd gotten as a waitress for seven years. It was never going to get it. My mother and grandmother Betty were two women who never asked questions and simply nodded yes with a profound knowledge.

I left the larger institution of universities and college campuses that I'd used to rise out of poverty at that point. After a few years in the poor house, it turned out to be a really good decision—perhaps the most daring feminist act I will ever commit, and one that resulted in dreams coming true. The underprivileged ladies in my blood gave me the courage I needed. A woman who knows her worth should sometimes lean in. But there are moments when she should just leave.

Parton would become well acquainted with the friction between those two techniques as Porter Wagoner's young female co-star on a show bearing his name.

Wagoner, who had a string of country singles in the 1950s, was a savvy businessman who capitalised on the new television medium before most musicians did. Born in a small town in southern Missouri's Ozarks, he was a self-made guy with an ego that rivalled his rhinestone-encrusted Nudie Cohn outfits. He was a commanding physical presence, standing tall with a long face, yellow pompadour, and solemn manner. Dolly, on the other hand, stood five feet tall and wore demure outfits with a bright, genuine grin. Parton would later become recognized for her showy appearances, but during Wagoner's performance, it's evident that he was the one who was more concerned with his image.

Wagoner was her father's age, but Parton had been hired as the variety show's equivalent of a romantic lead. She was supposed to be the lovely lady by his side, singing duets in which a guy and a woman play lovers. Wagoner, on the other hand, would get more than he bargained for.

Audiences were initially suspicious of Parton replacing prior female co-star Norma Jean, but she quickly became more popular than the host. Both she and Wagoner released solo albums in addition to the duets, and hers sold more than his. They both wrote songs, but hers was superior.

According to Parton's memoirs, the more threatened Wagoner felt, the tighter he tried to control Parton and her career—telling her what she should sing, what she should write, whether she was allowed to compose, and who would publish the songs. Parton wrote in her book about being frightened of conflict. When Wagoner didn't get his way, he was a blustery screamer, and she was a calm strength; he was a tortured soul who needed to be puffed up, and she was a stable, compassionate friend willing to sacrifice and give a lot. Theirs had all the hallmarks of an abusive relationship.

Wagoner did everything he could to keep other male business influences out of her life, straight out of the controlling-man playbook. He barred her uncle Billy Owens, her musical mentor and industry advocate for years. He recommended Adele leave her close friend and producer Fred Foster at Monument Records for RCA, where Wagoner served as a middleman. Yes, he wanted her to succeed, and her success aided him. But as her star soared, he became more competitive and possessive.

He draped his long arm around her petite shoulders during a television interview they made together in 1971, which is now available online, and commanded her when to speak—a jealous-boyfriend tactic many women would recognize.

Parton claims they had no intimate involvement and has never accused him of sexual harassment. However, romantic rumours concerning male and female co-stars inevitably abound. Parton hinted in her autobiography that Wagoner may have promoted the rumours. Tammy Wynette stood in for Parton on the show on occasion, and Parton recalled Wynette's anxiety about Wagoner's ability to tarnish both of their reputations with his tales of sexual conquest.

"One day I was talking to Tammy and she asked me, 'What if Porter claims we all slept with him?'" Parton penned the piece. " 'Don't be concerned, Tammy,' I said. 'Half of the people will think he's lying, and the other half will just think we have awful taste,' says the author.

Parton may have smiled through Wagoner's power plays, but a close examination of their on-screen banter reveals a lady who understands exactly what is going on and will respond to any slight with a subtle move capable of shredding Wagoner's thin veneer of elegance.

"You wanna put your guitar away and we'll sing a duet, or you wanna just keep it?" Wagoner requests a segue into a duet in which he will play guitar. His tone seems more like a command than an inquiry.

"I'll just hang onto it," Patron adds, as if to say, "nah, I'm fine, you son of a bitch."

"Okay," Wagoner says, forcing a smile.

"I need a security blanket," Parton continues, attempting to draw a line of self-preservation. The pair then sing "Her and the Car and the Mobile Home," from their 1972 duet album The Right Combination—Burning the Midnight Oil. The song is about an unfaithful husband who returns home to discover that his suffering wife has left him for good.

During the same episode, Wagoner makes a joke she doesn't like when introducing Parton's solo performance. She responds from behind the camera, jokingly disputing what he's stated. His broad smile fades for a split second.

"Shut up," he says bluntly, before breaking into Parton's enduring classic "Tennessee Mountain Home."

Perhaps it's no accident that Wagoner's aggressiveness is on full show in that 1972 episode—the year Parton's five-year contract with him expired.

Wagoner persuaded Parton to extend her contract, but the friction between them only grew. In one especially tense interaction during a 1973 episode, the discomfort of which Rolling Stone investigated in 2016, the nice girl Wagoner hired is now a tough woman on the verge of giving up.

"We're back again," Wagoner adds, placing his arm around Parton's shoulders. "This is me and my sidekick. She simply kicked me in the groyne." They both smile and giggle as Wagoner flinches and gasps as if Parton has struck him.

Parton turns around and stares up at him. "Not yet, but I think I will after that," she said.

Wagoner's arm pulls away from her, and his smile fades—this time for more than a split second.

"Ohhh," he mutters. "If you ever hit me and I find it out, Dolly Parton, you'll be in trouble."

They're then laughing and bobbing their way through the conversational duet "Run That by Me One More Time," in which a man lies about where he's been and a woman lies about how much money she spent.

Wagoner invites someone from the audience to join them onstage at the end of the song. Jimmy Dean, the country musician, enters the shot as a lumbering blue suit with his arms outstretched, heading for Parton. He pushes himself onto Parton as she giggles and pushes back, keeping their torsos apart for an uncomfortably long time. Parton had held her own in a verbal fencing duel against Wagoner, only to be physically attacked by a man whose name was synonymous with sausage.

Parton's bravery and chutzpah in those occasions may be lost on us today. She had avoided a life of physical labour, but her presence in male-dominated environments came with few safeguards. Perhaps it's a good thing she married soon after coming to Nashville; while many guys would mistreat a single woman, others might avoid pestering one who wears a wedding band, whether because she's "claimed" or because they're afraid of a whoopin' from her husband.

Wagoner, on the other hand, was Parton's spouse in the public eye, and the same stubbornness that drove him insane helped him make a fortune. Wagoner states in his speaking voice near the close of the studio version of "Run That by Me One More Time," "I ought to box your jaws." Parton answers, "Aw, you'd hit your mama first before you hit me."

This comic boldness in the face of an unfunny danger is a trademark of female country music and working-class women's culture. My grandmother Betty, you may recall, had her jaw smashed by an enraged husband as she was leaving him. He was her third ex-husband, she was twenty-three, destitute, and had two children. She laughed as she told me about it.

"Feel this," she whispered, lowering her chin and placing my hand on it. I felt her lower jaw slide to one side, and it produced a loud click, slightly out of place as it had been for nearly fifty years. "That was a gift from one of my sweethearts."

Betty, like so many other women, has lived a life that the more fortunate classes describe as "like a country song"—a backward interpretation. Parton and other artists purposefully told the tales of women they knew who were otherwise voiceless in society. To put it another way, the living preceded the music. Parton has never shied away from representing them, whether through her words or as a woman. On Wagoner's show, she'd turn out to be the woman in "Her and the Car and the Mobile Home" who eventually steals the trailer.

People can be found packing up and leaving in the lyrics of several music genres, but the departure in country music is notably impoverished, feminine, and American. You may compare the woman in these songs to the rambling male criminal who sings about gambling, honky-tonks, and trains.

Those men's lyrics frequently state that a lady is waiting for them at home, wonderfully tolerating her mate's mistreatment. My rough-hewn women are more like the one from the early 1990s. Lorrie Morgan's song "Watch Me" (also written by males) informs a dubious partner that she will leave, and you can tell by her voice which of them is correct. In "Wrong Side of Memphis," Trisha Yearwood drives a 1969 Tempest down Highway 40 toward Nashville to pursue her childhood ambition of performing at the Opry because she has nothing to lose. Such deviations are enabled given the personal liberties and geographic expanses of the United States, which are more commonly associated with male experiences.

Leaving affects the larger world of roots music as well. Tracy Chapman, in her two biggest singles, asks for one good reason to stay and plans to leave a harsh life behind with a fast automobile and some money she saved working at the convenience store.

The working-class woman is less tied to place than the middle-class woman, whose more solid, rooted existence includes a good job, a gym membership, and a position of leadership in community organisations. The impoverished lady will have a more difficult time getting money to go, but in spirit, she is what they term a flight risk, and what she longs to flee from is more than just a bad man. It's a little town, a difficult job, and an entire class.

In "Boston Town," bluegrass band Della Mae portrays one of the women who participated in the famous 1912 Bread and Roses Strike in Lawrence, Massachusetts, where nearly thirty thousand ethnically diverse textile workers, the majority of whom were female immigrants, banded together to expose dangerous working conditions and demand better wages.

"They said what a waste of a pretty girl / to let the labour flag unfurl," the lyrics to the song read. "I said, what more can you take from me? / I own my hands and my dignity."

"Boston Town" is a rare celebration of working-class female grit at the heart of social change, as are many of Parton's early songs. She simply tells them on the ground, in women's hearts and homes.

Parton's early songs also depict the woman who has not yet been liberated, the point just before advancement. These aren't stories about vehicles and horizons, but rather sombre, minor-key acknowledgements of situations from which a lady might need to flee. Young Parton sings over and over about women who are oppressed culturally and economically.

Parton's first RCA hit, "Just Because I'm a Woman," in 1968, highlighted the sexual double standards that encouraged males to be playboys while morally incriminating the women who slept with them. The song has a conventional country guitar twang, yet the concepts Parton pushed through Nashville in the lyrics were as subversive as feminist writings from academics and radical small presses.

In response to a disappointed partner's reprimand, the song portrays "slut shaming" long before the word was coined: "Yes I've made mistakes, but listen and understand / My mistakes are no worse than yours just because I'm a woman."

Parton then sings about a woman's destroyed reputation and her sexual partner abandoning her to propose to a virgin "angel."

Parton has stated that the inspiration for the song came from her own life. In her memoirs, she stated that she grew up pushing the bounds of acceptable behaviour in the devout backwoods of Tennessee, a place where smudging a charred matchstick across her lashes as eyeliner was scandalous.

When she met a lovely man named Carl Dean at a washing facility in Nashville shortly after arriving, he knew they were meant to marry. He also felt that a woman as lovely as Dolly had to be a "nice girl."

Eight months after their wedding, he started to inquire about her previous relationships.

"I assumed it didn't matter," she said in 2009 to Entertainment Weekly. "… I figured the truth was better, because I didn't want to start a marriage with a lie." He was shattered by the reality, and he cried over it for months.

"He could not get over that for the longest time," she told Rolling Stone in 2003. "I thought, 'Well, my goodness, what's the big damn deal?'"

The song she got out of that marriage argument, "Just Because I'm a Woman," reached the Top 20 chart in South Africa a few years after its US debut, much to her delight. In the Rolling Stone profile, she exclaimed, "All those oppressed women!"

With the title tune of her 1975 release "The Bargain Store," which Wagoner co-produced with Bob Ferguson at RCA, Parton continued to question the false saint-or-whore dichotomy. A woman compares herself to stuff that has been used and even broken but is still in good enough shape in the song, a haunting but self-assured plea from a woman to her would-be boyfriend. The strong chorus may allude to more than just an open heart: "The bargain store is open—come inside."

In an interview with Entertainment Weekly, Parton recalled that "a lot of stations wouldn't play it because they thought it was about a whore." Despite this, the single rose to become her fifth number-one solo hit.

The Fairest of Them All, Parton's 1970 album recorded around halfway through her stint on The Porter Wagoner Show, is composed of Parton originals that bore witness to the atrocities faced by women who are at the physical and economic whim of men and their ambitions. Of course, the album title alludes to a sexist fairy tale; on the cover, Parton smiles into a mirror with the fresh face of Snow White, but her long ruff alludes to the wicked queen.

In "Daddy Come and Get Me," an adult daughter asks her father to take her from a mental institution where her husband has placed her in order for him to be with another woman. That song shone light on the centuries-old practice of labelling a sane woman "crazy" and institutionalising her when it suited a man's purpose, a phenomena that was still prevalent in psychiatry in the 1970s.

On the third track of Fairest, a lady tells her partner that if he tries to change or control her, she will leave. "When possession gets too strong," Parton sings, "I'll be movin' on."

In "I'm Doing This for Your Sake," a woman's heart falls as she tells a newborn that she must put the baby up for adoption because the father fled away; to get her in bed, he promised her they'd be married and then split when he found out she was pregnant.

"Down from Dover," the album's songwriting highlight, sounds like 1970s pop-country: steel guitar, tambourine, backup vocals, and a bit of harpsichord laid against a mid-tempo melody. But it's typical Parton storytelling from her early career, when the ghosts of the women's fates she's averted are still hot on her tail. In the story, a teenage girl becomes pregnant and her parents ridicule her and kick her out of the house. The baby's father has left town, promising to return to marry her before she starts showing. She begs the youngster to return, but the seasons change without a word. In the autumn, she gives birth to a stillborn daughter without medical assistance: "I guess in some strange way she knew she'd never have a father's arms to hold her / And dying was her way of telling me he wasn't coming down from Dover."

Parton has stated that the song is still one of her favourites, and it has been sung by Marianne Faithfull and Nancy Sinatra. Just a few years ago, she was smiling and swaying to "Dumb Blonde," a song written by a male that conveyed some sass but lacked the gravitas Parton carried with her from the hollers of Sevier County. She was now narrating gothic stories about women that were too true to be broadcast on the radio. Parton recalled that RCA refused to release "Dover" as a single because of its contentious issue of unwed pregnancy.

She'd composed the song when she was just eighteen, she'd told crowds when debuting it, but society wouldn't be ready to hear her sing it until she was in her thirties.

"It was just a story about a girl having a baby—nothing really out of the ordinary about that," she told a London audience in 1983. "She thought somebody loved her, he left her in trouble, and never came back—but that seemed to be too heavy at the time."

Parton had left home for the bright lights of Nashville in the 1960s and 1970s and found success. But, in other respects, she was stuck in the same way she would have been as a beaten-up youngster in a cabin in Sevier County. She was one of the few female country music singers at the time, all of whom were produced and managed by guys in suits. It was such a man's world that she took up golf to stay in touch with them.

According to her autobiography, she once struck a birdie on a par three hole and was so pleased with herself that she had the Titleist ball mounted. Wagoner said he'd do it and then handed her a plaque without the unique golf ball—instead, it was an Arnold Palmer ball. Parton called the incident one of his numerous passive-aggressive jabs.

Back in the woods, Parton hadn't been shackled by a thoughtless boy and a teen pregnancy. Instead, she was professionally and contractually attached to a guy who pretended to be her spouse, parent, and owner. In some respects, he was her male counterpart—a talented, tenacious country kid with a guitar who worked hard and made it huge. What she'd walked into was a wealthier, showbiz version of the life she'd intended to flee. Her songs from that time period don't reflect the victory of an individualistic woman who "got out," but rather the sufferings of women who weren't so fortunate—a powerful statement of sympathy with her poor sisters back home, but also perhaps a hidden disclosure about her time with Porter Wagoner.

Parton's bus may have passed through women's protests, marches, and sit-ins as she toured the country singing those songs. Parton was unfamiliar with the world of direct political activism, knowing one's own agency in democracy, data and testimonials used to influence public policy. She knew what my grandmother Betty knew: female life is a personal, private experience in which an inner vibration you've been ignoring can jolt you so hard you'll fall to pieces if you don't leave.

That knowledge will be suppressed by society since women who do not stay put cannot be controlled. If they stay, all of the institutions benefit: They carry laundry baskets and emotional labour for the heterosexual marriage. Underpaying positions in which they complete their given work while also being required to organise the birthday cupcakes in the conference room. The parenting, in which they still change the majority of the diapers regardless of who "brings home the bacon"—and fry the majority of the bacon as well.

"Stay," her little town presumably told Parton when she left Tennessee in 1964, even if it was just by urging her to become a bride and mother and laughing at her great dreams of becoming a celebrity. "Stay," Porter Wagoner instructed her in plain legal words a decade later. That is, in many ways, the message for women everywhere. Today, however, we can rejoice in songs about leaving—music that depict stories that feel conceivable because of the exits made by women before us.

The leaving of a woman is a declaration. Many of them, particularly by poor women, Black women, brown women, homosexual women, and transgender women, have gone unnoticed as more fortunate people preach equality from microphones adjacent to capital buildings.

Dolly Parton was using a different type of microphone, and a young woman named Betty was listening. When I was a kid, I discovered Grandma Betty's old records, scrawled in ink with last names I had no idea she'd ever had. I was a child with plans to go, and no one in my family or rural towns ever laughed or tried to convince me that I couldn't. Nobody mentioned "feminism" where I lived. But the unfortunate females who came before me had already carved a rut on the road.

Parton's years with Wagoner remind me of the first line of Adrienne Rich's renowned 1978 poem, "A wild patience has taken me this far." In that poem, written by one of the country's most eminent public intellectuals and second-wave feminists, the middle-aged speaker realises her deepest strength is that she possesses seemingly contradictory qualities at the same time: anger and tenderness, a sad past and hope for the future, both pride and pain from having done a lifetime's worth of work alone.

How can patience be so ferocious? It's a query similar to, "Why did you put up with it?" The latter implies that a powerful lady would not. However, practically every woman must, at least momentarily.

Parton's business connection with Wagoner has provided her with financial stability. Of course, she was grossly underpaid. But, like many working women today, she was grateful and surprised to get paid at all.

"The jingles were sung, smiles were faked, and checks were cashed," Parton wrote in her autobiography. "Imagine what 60,000 dollars meant to a young woman who had grown up in poverty in the Smoky Mountains. It was certainly more than my father had ever earned in his life."

Parton redecorated her parents' house with new furniture, draperies, and carpet for her first Christmas after landing a job on Wagoner's show. Her younger siblings remained at home, and she made certain that the girls got many of the pink and frilly items that Parton had desired as a child. This concept of "girl stuff" may anger feminists. Parton's problem was not that such things were pushed on her, but that she couldn't have them. Pink ruffles were not simply a gender trap, but an economic luxury in a region where women worked alongside men, with little money for makeup or gowns even if they wanted them.

(For the record, the first big purchase she claims she made for herself after becoming completely affluent was not girly items. It was a car—not a Chevy approved by her husband, but a Cadillac she preferred.)

Grandma Betty never became wealthy or even "comfortable," but her career in the Kansas criminal justice system finally supplied enough to meet her expenditures as a little pension built. She always wore an emerald ring when I was a kid, and one day I asked her who had given it to her.

"I've had it since I started working in the courts," she said to me. "I always wanted an emerald ring, so I bought the damn thing myself." She didn't have to explain the significance—that every previous ring she'd put on a finger had been given to her by a guy.

Parton gained more than just financial security from her appearance on Wagoner's show. She received honours in both their names, including the Country Music Association's award for vocal group of the year in 1968. When Wagoner wanted to be, he could be a powerful champion for her. Though their relationship became tense, it had its ups and downs.

Wagoner organised "Dolly Parton Day" in her hometown of Sevierville in 1970, attracting renowned Nashville musicians to the occasion. The show was taped for the crucial live CD A Real Live Dolly. Of course, Wagoner benefited from that seemingly unselfish dedication to Parton and her roots, but she claims he also had true fondness and respect for her. It was a two-way street.

"He was a Missouri boy with a dream," she said in her memoir. Their life paths were so uncommon that they understood each other as few others could understand either of them.

Wagoner has the potential to be an excellent instructor as well. She'd been working professionally for nearly twenty years by the time they became partners. She still had a lot to learn about entertaining a national audience.

"I knew I could sing when I met Porter," Parton writes. "After knowing him, I knew how to perform."

He taught her how to deal with an audience's commotion; you can still see his imprint on a Parton concert today when someone disrupts a peaceful moment with a shout and she responds with a line.

Parton may have gotten her flair for rhinestones and over-the-top hair from Wagoner as well; she has long been seen in a Nudie costume.

The most important impression Wagoner made on her, however, was with fans.

"Every night after performing on the road, no matter how small the town or seemingly insignificant the venue, Porter would stay and sign autographs until the last fan who wanted one had been satisfied," Parton said in the book.

As it turned out, it was during one of those specialised signing sessions that she had an experience that led to her decision to leave Wagoner. A young girl, perhaps nine or ten years old, brought out a piece of paper for signature. Parton admired her auburn-coloured hair.

"You sure are pretty," Parton remembered responding. "What's your name?"

"Jolene," the girl introduced herself.

Parton had never heard of the person. She remembered it a year later when she sat down to write a song inspired by her husband's flirty relationship with an auburn-haired woman who worked at their bank. She needed a name for the character of the woman who was a menace to her. The moniker she chose, which she got from a young fan she met on the road with Wagoner, had such a ring to it that countless musicians across genres would cover the song for decades.

The 1973 single "Jolene" reached number one on the country charts, was a crossover pop hit, and received a Grammy nomination. It wasn't her first solo success, but something felt different about this one.

Parton felt more confident. She'd been patient with Wagoner for years, but she'd never lost her wild side. Despite their broad smiles on camera and onstage, the couple had gone around in circles behind the scenes.

"That was not unique to Porter," wrote Parton. "I had seldom agreed with parents, teachers, anybody who tried to exercise control over me, my talents, and my beliefs."

Finally, they had opposing visions: he wanted to retain her, and she didn't want to be kept.

"I guess the real problems that arose between Porter and me were all about duelling dreams," Parton stated in an email. "Porter dreamed of me staying with his show forever, and I dreamed of having my own show."

She had been with the show for seven years by that point, two years past her five-year contractual requirement, presumably out of loyalty to a man who believed she owed him her career. Parton isn't one to grumble or comment on her connection with Wagoner as anything more than a blessing that occasionally felt like a pain in the a$$. Her jokes about those years, like the songs she wrote at the time, are grim.

"Looking back, it seems appropriate," she said of her time with Wagoner. "After all, the indentured servants who came to the New World had to work seven years for their freedom."

So, in her late twenties, a decade after leaving rural East Tennessee, she found the courage to quit something that no longer served her needs. They were on tour as the long-running duo, Parton recalls in her memoir. A taxi was waiting for her in front of the hotel, with the door open.

"My knees nearly buckled, my heart nearly stopped, but I walked on," she wrote in the letter.

"I knew it was the end of an era when that car door closed." One Dolly Parton had walked so painfully to the automobile and climbed inside, while another, stronger one had shut the door."

One of her anxieties was that RCA would no longer want her. Wagoner, acting as a go-between, had successfully implied that the label wasn't interested in her without him. She requested a meeting in New York with executives Ken Glancy and Mel Ilberman.

"I know I'm not the same without Porter," she said, "but I'll be something really special by myself." They were taken aback, according to Parton.

"We're somewhat interested in maintaining a relationship with Porter Wagoner, but we think you are the real star," they were quoted as saying.

It's difficult to fathom a lady who has built a commercial empire feeling so insecure. It's not surprising, then, that she didn't realise the world respected her as much as she treasured herself. Years of input from an emotional manipulator like Wagoner will do a number on your mind, no matter how strong you are.

Parton wrote the tearjerker parting song "I Will Always Love You" for Wagoner to mark her departure from the show.

A song this strong isn't written until every word is true. But think what that kind of goodbye meant. Parton, no dummy, had long formed a song publishing firm and retained the rights anytime her work was recorded. Thus, her painful parting was something she owned and Wagoner had no claim to. Every penny it made ended up in her account, not his.

Parton spent her first summer apart from Wagoner on the road, opening for country artist Mac Davis. I picture her driving down the highway with her new band, Gypsy Fever, on a bus painted with butterflies and "Dolly" on the side. Don Warden, the famed steel guitarist from Wagoner's birthplace who had been a part of his act and original trio, could have been riding along. He and Parton had grown close; when she left Wagoner, he followed, becoming her manager for nearly a half-century.

Parton must have had a new sense of freedom as the bus flew past a field she wasn't working in and a café where she would never have to wait tables. She was twenty-eight years old and, for the first time in her life, she was free, with no location, man, or contract tying her wings. I picture "I Will Always Love You" playing on the bus radio, with the Gypsy Fever musicians ecstatic as the DJ reveals it has reached number one on the charts. I imagine Carly Simon's 1972 classic "You're So Vain" playing next, and Parton singing along, laughing her head off at one line in the chorus: "I'll bet you think this song is about you, don't you?"

Parton was overjoyed when Elvis Presley invited her to record "I Will Always Love You," she told CMT in 2006. She was already a star, but Presley was already a legend. Then, right before the recording session, Presley's manager, "Colonel" Tom Parker, attempted a business ruse on her.

"He said, 'Now you know we have a rule that Elvis don't record anything that we don't take half the publishing,'" Parton was quoted as saying by CMT. "And I was very quiet." 'Well, now it's already a hit,' I said. I authored it and it's already been published. And this is what I'm leaving behind for my family when I die."

Parker reminded her that it was either a deal or no deal.

"I guess they thought since they already had it prepared and already had it ready, that I would do it," Parton said with a laugh. "'I'm really sorry,' I said, and I cried all night."… Others were saying, 'You're insane. This is Elvis Presley. I mean, I'd give him anything."

But Parton went with her gut. It would prove one of the most lucrative decisions of her life.

"I Will Always Love You" went to number one again when Parton re-recorded it in 1982, making it the only country song in history to top the charts in two separate decades. The song did it a third time, in 1992, when Whitney Houston made it a pop blockbuster on The Bodyguard soundtrack. Thus, Parton's parting gift to the man who would have held her down ended up one of the most successful songs in music history. She is still cashing the checks.

"When Whitney's [version] came out, I made enough money to buy Graceland," Parton told CMT with a laugh.

The confidence to heed her inner voice and, in doing so, piss off a powerful man is what allowed Parton to leave Wagoner, say no to Elvis, and become not just a successful artist but also a business juggernaut.

"You need to really believe in what you've got to offer, what your talent is—and if you believe, that gives you strength," Parton told Billboard magazine in 2014. "In my early days, I would go in, and I was always over-made, with my boobs sticking out, my clothes too tight, and so I really looked like easy prey to a lot of guys—just looked easy, period. But I would go in, and if they were not paying close attention to what I was saying, I always said, 'I look like a woman, but I think like a man and you better pay attention or I'll have your money and I'll be gone.'"

Gone she was, and Wagoner responded with a bitter lawsuit. He claimed that, having played such a big role in her development, he was owed a cut of every profit she'd make for the rest of her life as an entertainer. That might seem like a losing claim today, but Parton had fair reason for concern as a woman facing the prospect of a courtroom with a male judge. Rather than fight Wagoner in court, Parton offered to settle for a reported $1 million. Wagoner took the deal.

According to Parton's book, she didn't yet have that amount lying around and paid it off painstakingly over time. Meanwhile, Wagoner was slandering her any chance he could get.

"Dolly Parton is the kind of person that I would never trust with anything of mine," Wagoner told a TV interviewer in 1978. "I mean her family, her own blood, she would turn her back on to help herself. I'm not that kind of person." In spite of this, according to multiple sources, she sometimes bailed him out of tax trouble.

Parton and Wagoner would reconcile and reunite many times over the decades, even poking fun at their history together. At a 1995 roast of Wagoner, Parton told the crowd, "I knew he had balls when he sued me for a million dollars when he was only paying me thirty dollars a week."

Parton would continue to reflect on Wagoner with a mix of straight talk and gracious thanks over the years.

"I will always be grateful to Porter, because I learned a lot," she told Rolling Stone in 2003. "But he got as much out of me as I got out of him, let's put it that way. Porter was very much like my dad and my brothers and the men I grew up with. They were just manly men, and a woman's place was where you told her to be. And so I would always stand up to him.... And we fought like hell, and he showed his ass about it, rather than just letting life flow. He had to sue me. And, of course, that broke both our hearts. And, you know, looking back on it now, he hates that he did that and has said so."

Parton and Wagoner might have buried the hatchet, but even his 2007 obituary in the New York Times revealed Wagoner's selfish nature:

"For all Mr. Wagoner's accomplishments, he could not escape a certain question. 'Did you sing with Dolly?' too many people asked.

"'No,' he would say with a smile. 'She sang with me."

PUNCHING OUT

Feminist activism was transforming the globe while Parton was leaving Wagoner. In 1973, the Supreme Court issued its decision on Roe v. Wade, which may have rescued many of the young, pregnant, abandoned characters of Parton's early songs. The following year, unpaid maternity leave became prohibited, and the Women's Educational Equity Act provided funding for the production of less sexist teaching materials.

While many of those improvements have lasted, the United States did not emerge as a bright and easy place for women. For decades, reproductive rights have been the target of death-by-a-thousand-cuts political methods.

Similarly, despite being free of her ties to Wagoner, Parton did not have a happy ending. A woman can escape the destitute countryside and a domineering male boss, but she can't leave a sexist and misogynistic culture. With some success, reject it mindfully every day? Perhaps. Exist in the absence of it? No.

To say nothing of the fights she undoubtedly fought behind closed doors, Parton's songwriting would continue to enrage powerful men long after the seeming end of equality. Her 1991 song "Eagle When She Flies," a ballad she created to pay homage to women's simultaneous vulnerability and inner power, had the same difficulty getting on the airwaves as "Down from Dover" and "The Bargain Store" had a quarter century before.

"A lot of DJs wouldn't play [it] because they thought it was such a feminist song," Parton told Rolling Stone in 2003.

Parton's refusal to apply the name "women's lib" to her own work reveals where she came from. However, the fact that men determined her music should not be played reveals exactly what it was.

Parton's reaction to male DJs who play "Eagle When She Flies": She sang it at the Country Music Association Awards in front of President George H. W. Bush and First Lady Barbara Bush. She used the occasion to introduce her song by contrasting what she wished to elevate with the ultimate icon of patriarchy—the affluent, white, male leader of the world.

"Everyone was saying how proud they were to have the president here. And so we are. I am extremely honoured. But I wanted to sing a song tonight and dedicate it to Barbara Bush," Parton remarked, her platinum wig nearly as high as some of her old beehives and her neckline considerably lower than Porter Wagoner would have approved. "We all know there are some wonderful men in the world, but there are just as many wonderful women." She and others like her, as well as women from all walks of life.... So this is for all the women here tonight and around the world."

The stage was lit up to reveal a large, mostly white choir dressed in cheesy outfits representing professional trades that women were just entering—the businesswoman in shoulder pads, the delivery driver in a brown jumpsuit holding a box, the soldier in fatigues, the astronaut, policewoman, surgeon, construction worker, and even a movie director. The jobs historically held by women were also present: the teacher, the nurse, the rancher, and the restaurant waitress with her tray. However, the president of the United States of America, who had everything handed to him whereas Parton had to work for it, had to consider the visuals. Captive in front of cameras, he watched as the daughter of an uneducated farmer informed him his wife was his equal. It was an amazing performance that, despite its absurd images, nevertheless feels revolutionary when viewed now.

That was about thirty years after Parton departed Sevierville, Tennessee, with a guitar as a youngster. Sexual discrimination in the workplace was illegal at the time of the CMA Awards performance, and more women were recording country music. Women have made considerably greater progress since then in many areas. But some of us get so caught up in the ideological debates around feminism that we fail to take a hard look at how we live our lives. What kind of country music could be written about us? Would they be about the trapped lady or the one bursting free?

You may know a well-to-do lady with a college degree and a nice, philandering husband who covers the bills but treats her like a trophy or a maid regardless of whether she has her own work. She might be content enough in her life to stay. She might even wear a "feminist" T-shirt to pick up her husband's dry laundry. She might understand terms that a poor woman cannot, and she might write an upset Facebook post against our misogynist president.

Meanwhile, a poor mother walks out a door with nothing to her name, hoping to get some goddamn respect for herself and her children. Behind closed doors, the woman who preaches about feminism is not often the one who actually insists for equality.

Leaving was a revolutionary move, whether it was destitute Dolly Parton refusing to stay in a holler or wealthy Dolly Parton looking at the door of Porter Wagoner's studio. It is a power that has dragged textile mills, coal firms, and wealthy corporations to their knees over the years when gender and poverty collide, and working women have had enough.

As a child, I remember being enthralled with an episode of Roseanne in which the title character stands up to a sexist, physically abusive employer who then breaks his word and reinstates punishing production quotas for female employees at a small-town Illinois plastics firm.

"You're staying... "And so will your loser friends," her boss says. Roseanne dashes out to the manufacturing floor after some heated comments.

"Hey, I'm not done with you!" he exclaims as he pursues her to where the other women are rearranging plastic pieces. "Roseanne, I thought I told you not to walk away from me."

"I'm walking away from you forever," she adds softly, as if afraid. "I'm leaving this disgusting factory." "I'm leaving this terrible job." Roseanne clocks in and out.

"Well, that was a wonderful performance, Roseanne," he said. "If any of you are thinking about joining her, I'd like to point out that there are two doors to this room." One pays, the other does not."

Her pals of various races and ages step up and punch their cards one by one.

When Dolly Parton punched her card and walked out of the Porter Wagoner music factory, she was paving the way for female performers in an industry where women were still rarely the headliner.

"There was Patsy Cline, Loretta Lynn, Tammy Wynette, and me," Parton explained to Rolling Stone. "There were just very few of us, and they were all under the direction of men."

"Dolly & Loretta & Patsy & Tammy," the shirt reads.

If you see it, consider it a reminder to tip the next woman who serves you at a diner like the ones on the Great Plains where my grandmother waited tables, or to the cleaning lady carrying a bucket on and off Greyhound buses like Cline did down South. Feminism owes her a debt, and she's probably saving money to get anywhere. Hers isn't the kind of life you want to be a part of.

CHAPTER 3

DOLLY PARTON BECOMES THE BOSS

In the 1980 film 9 to 5, three frustrated women confront their male supervisor, who berates, gropes, and demeans them. The film provided for many viewers the first articulation and criticism of flagrantly, dangerously sexist office culture that had long been accepted as "the way things are" or "boys being boys." It was a fable conveying lessons for men and women alike.

It wasn't a leap for Dolly Parton to play the boss's objectified secretary. She had recently left The Porter Wagoner Show, where she had spent years working for one of Nashville's most prominent male egos.

"I know all about bosses from Porter Wagoner," Parton told Entertainment Weekly in 2009, after writing the score for the Broadway rendition of 9 to 5. "He was a male chauvinist pig too."

Perhaps this is why, of the three strong female leads—Parton, Jane Fonda, and Lily Tomlin—the least skilled actor, in my opinion, produces the most compelling performance.

Of course, Fonda and Tomlin were aware of sexism. And Tomlin, the daughter of a manufacturing worker who, like Parton's father, briefly left the South for steady work in Detroit, must have witnessed the interconnections of gender and economic conflict firsthand. But there's something glistening about Parton on-screen, and it's not just her frosted eye shadow.

It was because she was nearing the pinnacle of her career, when she would become not only a movie star, but also a business entrepreneur and global icon. She'd do it all while wearing a massive platinum-blonde wig, skin-tight clothes, and plenty of cleavage.

She was a third-wave feminist born a generation early, breaking gender stereotypes while indulging in gender performance before it became a political act. Country ladies like myself were on the lookout.

I recently saw 9 to 5 in an Austin, Texas, theatre full of ladies shouting at the screen. People think of the picture as a comedy, which is how I remembered it from watching it on TV as a youngster. But, as a woman, when Parton's character is physically grabbed by her boss, I felt a wave of trauma-triggered nausea wash over me. When the main characters fantasise about murder and put what they believe is their boss's dead body into the trunk of a car, the women in the audience cheered. It struck me as one of the darkest films ever done about the female experience.

It is also very applicable now. Thirty-six years after the film's premiere, the United States president embodies the vile male boss. Donald Trump, while appearing on a reality show in which he got a kick out of saying "you're fired," memorably told a female participant she would look fine on her knees. Contestants in the beauty pageants he ran said he had a habit of strolling in when they were changing their clothes. In contemporary times, 9 to 5 feels so political that one wonders if a big studio would approve it today.

Born the same year as 9 to 5, I am now almost the same age as Parton was when she acted in the picture. I'm also what they dubbed "a professional woman" during my 1980s youth and 1990s adolescence—financially independent since the age of eighteen by the sweat of my own brow, happily divorced and childless, more driven by job aspirations than home ones.

I've come to think of myself and other women my age as the cultural children of the 9 to 5 job. We grew up in a muddle of new social liberties and old expectations. Society was adopting a new idea of the modern woman: she went to work in the morning as a doctor, an engineer, or a police officer. But did she also enjoy baking? Of course, you can enjoy cooking, wearing high heels, and doing other stereotypically "feminine" things and still be a feminist. Today's mainstream culture appears to be unambiguous on this point. But the defining tension for women in the late twentieth century was being urged to become whatever they wanted while being chastised regardless of how they went about it. If they raced into male-dominated halls of business or government, their feminism transformed them into loud Amazons in the eyes of threatened men;

if they wore low-cut shirts and tight pants while making empowered judgments, their feminism was completely missed by threatened women.

The concept of gender equality at home and at work was so fresh at the time that a woman's entire existence may be viewed as a planned remedy to centuries of unfair treatment. In 1992, a little more than a decade after the release of 9 to 5, the first lady of Arkansas, a Yale Law School-educated attorney named Hillary Clinton, was chastised for explaining to reporters covering her husband's presidential campaign why she worked on public policy rather than draperies as the wife of a governor.

"I suppose I could have stayed home and baked cookies and had tea," Secretary of State Hillary Clinton said. "But what I decided to do was to fulfil my profession, which I entered before my husband was in public life." That comment, and the widespread pearl-clutching in response to it, would haunt her twenty-four years later, when she campaigned for president herself.

Clinton remarked sarcastically about baking cookies, not because she dislikes baking, but because for generations society has given women aprons while denying them social and political power. Parton portrayed herself as a "floozy" not because she desired men's approval, but because sexualizing herself removed authority away from guys who would otherwise have done it for her.

Women had little choice but to react to the herky-jerky social achievements that occurred at the conclusion of the last century. If one wants to fight a disadvantage, it is a paradox. The female leads in 9 to 5 aren't homicidal criminals by nature. They don't want to kill their boss. But they discover that they may have to.

According to original playwright Patricia Resnick, her earlier draft of the script was considerably more horrific. Resnick told Rolling Stone in a 2015 interview commemorating the film's 35th anniversary that she planned to make "a very dark comedy in which the secretaries actually tried to kill the boss." In order to make the three characters more likeable, certain plot points were reworked as fantasy sequences.

In terms of general casting, the fact that the lead females would all be white was probably not even questioned. Even today, a woman of colour rarely stars a film, let alone as a figure holding a gun at a white male boss.

Another item that hasn't changed is the movie's gender points. Resnick recounted talks with suspicious media when the film was transformed into a Broadway musical in 2009.

"It was really frustrating," she added, "because a lot of the interviews I did with male journalists, the first thing they said was, 'Well, none of those issues are a problem in contemporary life, so how are women of today going to be able to relate to it?'" I thought, well, you can't sexually harass someone as obviously. We do not refer to people as secretaries.' What else has changed?"

As a woman who has worked in the workforce for more than twenty years and has never—not once—worked somewhere where there was no harassment or other discrimination based on my gender, I must say that I agree. The constant emotional drain of being ignored, underpaid, ogled, and regarded as a threat is a big part of why I've given up the numerous perks and security of organisational structure to work as a freelance writer.

What's different for me and my generation than it was for our moms and grandmothers, as Resnick recounts, is that many of the men who have antagonised us in the workplace have done so in much quieter ways than 9 to 5's loud chauvinism—often while claiming to be "feminists." That can be an even more dangerous professional environment for women; subtle misogyny or sexism can cut you before you realise it and is the most difficult to prove.

Feminism, like all movements for social development, unavoidably has a gap between what's on paper and what's really going on: between feminism declared and feminism enacted, women's rights legislated and women's rights enforced, policy advancement and cultural progress. In meaningful ways, women of Generation X, of which I am a member, enjoyed greater independence than their moms. We were the first full beneficiaries of Title IX safeguards, which guaranteed equal access to school and prohibited sexual discrimination in the workplace. As the Violence Against Women Act became law, we were beginning our first romantic relationships. But the cultural cues we were given as children were riddled with gaps and discord.

I was recently surprised by an old episode of Moonlighting, a favourite childhood program that, in my memory, was a feminist victory for casting Cybill Shepherd as a whip-smart (and damn funny) detective. Bruce Willis' character, the grinning work partner with whom she has just concluded an on-again/off-again liaison, appears in her house against her will. He refuses to go when she tells him to, slaps her in the face for arguing with him, and is then welcomed into her arms for his tenacity.

My twentieth-century infant eyes had witnessed a strong woman fighting and then getting turned on by a man determined enough to win. My adult eyes saw a dangerously entitled man following a woman and not respecting or even believing her when she said "no."

That was the conundrum described by 9 to 5 at the start of the 1980s: a woman's new function in the economy at odds, in men's view, with her old role in bed. Female Baby Boomers had to deal with it, and their Generation X kids observed as they walked home in high heels, with little time to complain.

Those same problems harm women today and will continue to do so for future generations. However, 9 to 5 indicates a specific point of friction in the evolution of feminism: The Equal Rights Amendment had not yet been repealed, middle-class women were power-walking to work (as impoverished women had done for decades), and popular culture reflected a serious collective gender problem.

That decade of transition—from the Carter to the Reagan eras, from polyester bell bottoms to stone-washed denim, from women's-lib placards to the mistaken belief that liberation had occurred—marked an enormous transformation in Parton's career as well. After establishing herself as a solo country music artist in the 1970s, 9 to 5 catapulted her to mainstream Hollywood stardom and expedited her path to becoming an icon.

Parton never used her stardom to promote feminist marches or overt political activism. Among what must have been innumerable alternatives, she chose as her debut script a film developed by one of the most reviled women of the time—Jane Fonda, who was still a polarising figure with her antiwar "Hanoi Jane" dispute fresh in national memory. And Parton agreed to play a woman who lassos her violent boss and shoves a revolver in his face as her debut role.

It's no coincidence that Parton was ready to play Doralee, the attractive secretary who was sexually harassed by her nasty male employer and shunned by her female coworkers who propagated the false idea that she was sleeping with him.

Doralee's special ailment among the other mistreated female workers was being labelled a "slut" because of her seductive beauty and other men's fraudulent accusations of banging her. Parton got accustomed to it in high school.

"I put on a lot of makeup." I wore really tight clothes and my hair was a mile long. "I looked like the real trash that a lot of the girls were," Parton said on the Late Show with David Letterman in 1987. "A lot of those people thought I was a bad influence on their daughters because I made fun of them and wore a lot of makeup." Actually, I was quite decent. I simply had an outgoing personality. Some of the girls I was hanging out with were really into it, and I got all the credit."

FEMINIST SWEET SPOT

Despite the contradictory messages of the era, I consider myself fortunate to have grown up within the feminist sweet spot that followed the organised marches and policy victories of the 1970s but before the full-throated conservative response of the new millennium. Following Roe v. Wade, but before right-wing fanatics devised a successful strategic plan for undermining reproductive rights. After a large number of women entered traditionally male occupations, but before online trolls used technology to stalk, harass, and shame them. Before Fox News put their legs in the shot, female journalists began hosting national network shows.

Women my age—children and adolescents in the 1980s, teenagers and young women in the 1990s—may recall that era through songs, cassette cassettes, and television channel dials rather than adult politics. However, what we discovered through those records and TV shows frequently had a decidedly political undercurrent.

Our formative years came before the Spice Girls' and Britney Spears' hot-pink, baby-talk girl power, and before Beyoncé and the Dixie Chicks' overt, unabashed acceptance of the term "feminism." Instead, we had a series of tough women in pantsuits who ran intellectual circles around the men they worked with: Murphy Brown and Dana Scully. Connie Chung and Diane Sawyer give the evening news with huge, angular hairdos. Clair Huxtable and Angela Bower are stylish but tough-as-nails working moms in shoulder pads on their way out the door. Whitney Houston and Selena Gomez wore leather jackets and sang pop songs about streetwise sexual strength. Queen Latifah and Salt-N-Pepa rap for respect in baggy pants and sneakers. Shirley Manson and Sinéad O'Connor in combat boots, telling the world to fuck off.

Women in rhinestones and fringed leather sang triumphantly about hard-won independence in pop-country music, a genre increasingly linked with conservatism.

"Girls' Night Out" from the Judds' chart-topping 1984 first album, Why Not Me, was probably my mother's most frequently played vinyl record when I was a kid. It expresses relief at the end of a long work week. "I've been cooped up all week long / Workin' my fingers to the bone," the Judds croon over saloon piano and steel guitar. They're off to dance, party, and close down the country bar.

That's all. That's the entire song—fun for the sake of enjoyment, with no mention of finding a man.

K. T. Oslin states in 1987's "Younger Men," another popular song my mom played over and over in her car's tape system, that she had begun entertaining younger lovers. She recalls giggling as a young lady at a statistic stating that men reach their sexual optimum at the age of nineteen and women at the age of forty. As she sings, "Now I'm staring forty right in the face / And the only trouble with being a woman my age is the men my age."

My mother was only in her twenties when that album, 80's Ladies, was released. I was seven years old. But, as Mom drove down the road with a Marlboro Light in her hand and I bobbed my head in the passenger seat, we both enjoyed chatting along with the song's spoken aside. "Blue shorts, no shirt / WOOOO you're lookin' good, darlin'! / That's right—stay in shape," says Oslin, switching the normal gender roles of catcaller in the vehicle and catcalling on the sidewalk: "That's right—stay in shape."

We were singing along with that song once when we drove past a man jogging in blue shorts, and we both laughed—a delightful surge of empowerment surging through us from Oslin's songwriting pen to a damaged road in Kansas. I'm not sure how each of us felt about the unique power shift in a middle-aged woman singing those lines, but a twenty-something mom and her brilliant youngster did.

Parton was also in her forties at the time, and she had been ahead of her time in penning songs about sexual power. As the 1970s came to an end, she began to change her lyrics away from the broken, mistreated ladies of her previous career and toward uptempo songs like the pop-country hit "Two Doors Down" from the disco-infused 1978 album Here You Come Again.

The woman singing in the song is crying about something (probably a breakup), but she resolves to stop crying. She hears a rager down the corridor and moves in that direction. By the next stanza, she's inviting a new guy to her apartment. Parton goes on to sing, "Here we are feeling everything but sorry / We're having our own party two doors down."

Parton, who moved to Los Angeles in 1976, was undoubtedly affected by the sexual emancipation messages of the counterculture movement of the time. But, as a teenager in rural Tennessee, she reported having that same freedom and power—self-possession before society approved.

Parton's sexual experience was or was not restricted by monogamous marriage, which she married shortly after arriving in Nashville at the age of eighteen in 1964. ("I said I was married," she admitted to the New York Times in 2016. "I didn't say I was dead.") However, in the garish 1980s, she exaggerated and emphasised her looks in new ways, indicating a woman finally coming into her own, sexually. Her neckline was lowered, and her heels were raised.

After playing the misunderstood Doralee in 9 to 5, Parton co-starred in The Best Little Whorehouse in Texas with Burt Reynolds as the typical heart-of-gold sex worker. It's worth mentioning that she's no longer a worker bee in the brothel, but rather the queen. The metaphor of the oppressed working female, on the other hand, would always infuse her worldview.

"When I think somebody's acting more like a pimp than a manager, and I'm more of a prostitute than an artist, I always tell them where to put it," Parton said in a 2014 interview with Maclean's. "People will use you as long as you let them."

The feminism in Parton's music and image may have been lost on cultural commentators of the time, but it was hard to miss behind the scenes. Parton sought to meet firebrand Texas leftist Ann Richards, who was running for state treasurer at the time Best Little Whorehouse was released.

Photographer Scott Newman was filming a campaign event for Richards when they met at the historic Driskill Hotel in downtown Austin. He took a picture of the two women standing together: Richards, a progressive renowned for her outspoken feminism and great one-liners, and Parton, a new movie star recognized for her own version of the same thing.

The two women appear in profile in the black-and-white photograph, overcome with exuberant laughter and nearly mirror images but for the difference in age and body shape: blond, tight curls atop both their heads and ruffles on both their blouses.

"What a scene to witness!" Newman wrote in the notes for a recent photographic exhibition. "These two women, two of my all-time favourite human beings, took such delight in each other."

Parton and Richards would become great friends and were both on their way up: Parton to becoming a pop culture phenomenon and Richards to becoming the last woman and the last Democrat to rule the state of Texas as of this writing. Two separate journeys, yet two ladies who share a lot.

The Lone Star State, as well as country music and the country as a whole, have evolved dramatically in the more than three decades since that photograph was shot. Texas, like the rest of the country, has swung to the right; Ann Richards would not win a Texas campaign today. Meanwhile, Nashville has eschewed female political renegades such as the Dixie Chicks in favour of a bevy of male artists ranging from "bro country" Luke Bryan to old-school, bearded outlaw Chris Stapleton. Parton's new music was dropped from country radio decades ago. It's difficult to envision the Southern gothic defences of poor women she wrote in her twenties being broadcast now.

But there in that 1982 snapshot, taken in a Southern state capital, is a brief but profound moment in American history that girls like me— then a toddler living in a metal trailer on the Kansas prairie— somehow understood. A female politician and a female country-superstar-turned-Hollywood, sharing looks of mutual regard, throwing back their heads and laughing in a public place of power that reactionary twenty-first-century misogyny had yet to recover.

BODY POLITICS

Parton was forced to carry a hyper-awareness of her bodily shape and its relationship to the environment because of reactions to her physical appearance. Every woman suffers from male stares, but Parton's story demonstrates how invisible a woman's humanity can be when that look is a laser beam the size of the Earth.

When she appeared on Johnny Carson's Tonight Show in 1977, he fumbled and stated, "I have certain guidelines on this show, but I would give about a year's pay to peek under [her top]."

She couldn't even avoid being turned into a visual object by a blind man. In 1978, at the awards ceremony where she became the second woman ever to be crowned Country Music Association Entertainer of the Year (now one of seven in total), visually challenged singer Ronnie Milsap informed the audience, "I want to know why she wasn't in my braille Playboy." (Parton had been on the cover of the magazine that month in a rabbit suit but had declined to pose naked.)

Parton describes the pressures she faced during that time in her 1994 autobiography, Dolly, without mentioning the gendered component to all of them: male business associates who gave her bad advice, her siblings' resentment for her fame and fortune despite her generosity as a family caregiver, and Hollywood's sexist body-shaming.

Parton claimed that the shoot for Best Little Whorehouse was extremely terrible, citing the set's overall negative mood. Her petite but sensuous figure was deemed too small for the big screen. Parson's tale of being humiliated while filming take after take of a sequence in which Reynolds' character scoops her up and carries her over a threshold makes you cringe. In describing the event, she emphasises on her personal role in the scene, stating she felt like a failure because of her weight.

Parton's destitute beginnings, in which adversity and hunger shaped her brain, worsened her interaction with the already difficult issue of a woman's appetite and physical size.

"My daddy and mama just think I'm dying or something," Parton said to Chantal Westerman on Good Morning America in 1987, shortly after she grew considerably slimmer (much to the media's delight). "... 'If you're gaining weight, you're picking up,' my father usually says at home. And if you're losing weight, you're dropping.' 'Boy, you're falling off,' remarked Daddy. "You're still falling off, aren't you?"

Her father spent decades farming and building to ensure that his eleven surviving children did not starve to death. While Parton has stated that she is not underweight for a petite woman and that her "dramatic weight loss" in the 1980s was a shift to feeling more healthy rather than less healthy, a culture and family shaped by the Great Depression and even the European famines their ancestors fled will see shrinking size as cause for concern.

Meanwhile, as Carson and Milsap's quips show, culture's solution to the perplexing subject of Dolly Parton—a quick intellect, a gorgeous face, a creative genius, and a massive rack all rolled into one—was to make her the punch line of a joke about enormous tits.

That joke became so ingrained in the American psyche that I remember as a child on a playground in the 1980s seeing small boys put balls under their shirts and exclaim, "Look, I'm Dolly Parton." "What's this?" they'd ask, flipping their hands upside down and extending only the middle finger. (Answer: "Dolly Parton standing behind a tree.")

Parton recovered the joke; she frequently refers to her own bosom before anyone else does. She made a profession out of that kind of spirit. But gaining control of the forces that attempted to reduce her must have been a difficult emotional trip.

Parton had breast augmentation surgery not long after she "lost the weight" that decade, something she has mentioned in general terms in her book and elsewhere. Photos from her early career demonstrate that, while her breasts are now considered "fake," they are roughly the same size they were when they were "real." People find the resulting figure shocking—a petite woman with breasts that don't appear to match her size. But it stands to reason that a lady whose mere mention elicited boob jokes would reclaim not just the joke but the boob itself—as if to emphasise that no punch line had led her to feel ashamed.

When asked about the difficult juxtaposition of her origins in poverty, her profession as a musician and company owner, and her notoriety as a female sex symbol, Parton invariably grinned and chuckled. Such influences, however, take their toll, even on a lady who "made it" due to her natural tenacity.

It was a difficult time for the women who blazed the route Parton was on—a trail that was particularly obstructed and perilous for women of colour, homosexual women, and those who did not fit the cisgender, straight, white mould more palatable to American power structures. The decade was a jumble of contradictory messages for any woman on that path: Work a "man's job" but for less money. Wear shoulder pads to convey masculinity, but also high heels to click lightly down the corridor. Be self-sufficient enough to drive to work yet report to a man supervisor and make your husband's dinner when you both return home from work.

That jumble of expectations has changed little in the intervening thirty years, but it had a newness in the 1980s that spun American culture and drove even tough-as-nails Parton to crumble. Because she is everyone else's support system, such a lady frequently pays a high price. So, who looks after her?

Parton's darkest phase occurred in the early 1980s, when she was in her thirties: a physical and emotional breakdown during which she considered suicide. Her personal demise coincided with the anti-feminist backlash's first major win, the defeat of the Equal Rights Amendment in 1982.

Sandy Gallin, the late talent shepherd who also oversaw Michael Jackson's career, is mentioned in Parton's autobiography as a source of compassionate assistance to aid her through her serious depression. Parton eventually had to do what so many women do in order to live a life that suits herself rather than everyone else: burn it all down and rebuild.

Parton let go of some associates around that time, including band members and an accounting firm that kept forgetting that she made the decisions with her own money. She also had a partial hysterectomy, she revealed without explaining why. One positive outcome she has noticed is that she is no longer taking the high-oestrogen birth control pills that were on the market at the time. It was also a watershed event in her decision not to have children.

Parton recovered from her emotional breakdown by cleaning the house in her business, band, cupboards, bloodstream, and even her own womb. Her thinking became more optimistic, her body rebalanced, and her business began a crescendo that hasn't subsided since.

She didn't need to kill herself because she'd experienced what some cultures call a shamanic death, she said in her book. "By the grace of God," she said in her letter, "I had [died] without experiencing it in the actual physical sense."

Since youth, Parton has been deliberately, consciously evolving—from a poor country kid to a Nashville hopeful, from Porter Wagoner's micromanaged co-star to crossover solo artist, from small-screen singer to big-screen actor. Now that she'd attained the degree of fame and money she'd worked for her whole life, she'd hit rock bottom emotionally and found herself the same woman she'd always been—yet psychologically reborn. What is the next objective? She had conquered a man's world like only a woman could and discovered it to be a place that treated her like dirt even when she was on top. The only thing left to do was to make her own damn world.

WELCOME TO DOLLYWOOD

"I never got to go to Disneyland as a child, but I was always fascinated with it," Parton told Maverick magazine in 2011, twenty-five years after founding an amusement park in her home state of Tennessee. In the 1980s, as a homesick, freshly minted movie star dissatisfied with the Hollywood she had imagined as a youngster, Parton returned to the Smokies to establish Dollywood.

Dollywood was more than simply a selfish venture. It was her vision for reviving her hometown's poor rural economy and putting its inhabitants to work, including her own family members.

"I knew it would be a great place for all the hardworking, good-hearted, honest people in this area that don't have jobs," she told the newspaper. She envisaged it would be a happy place, full of fun, music, rides, craftsmanship, and culture from her home region.

"A lot of my business people said: 'That's a big mistake, that's a great way to lose all your money," Parton told Reuters in 2016. "But I had a gut feeling it was the right thing to do, so I went ahead with it." Then I fired the lawyers and accountants who didn't trust in me and hired new ones.``

Parton was now in charge, and her business instincts were correct. She told Reuters that Dollywood, which marked its 30th anniversary in 2016, is her most profitable investment. Every year, three million people visit. Parton's delight, and indeed the park's success, is enhanced by the fact that numerous generations of her family continue to work and perform at the attraction, just as she had envisioned.

Parton's aspirations for Dollywood's community effect were also realised. According to a study conducted this year by University of Tennessee academics, the Pigeon Forge, Tennessee, tourist magnet employs approximately 350 people and generates roughly 20,000 jobs in the area. Dollywood has a $1.5 billion annual economic impact on East Tennessee, according to the experts. (That is a billion.) If Parton had listened to those who questioned her business acumen, not only would she have lost money, but the entire state would have.

Parton managed to make one of the best collaborative albums of all time, Trio, with Emmylou Harris and Linda Ronstadt, while launching that venture. Trio earned a Grammy and topped the Billboard country albums chart with their superb harmonies and decidedly country sound.

Parton hosted a new ABC television show that same year. Parton was scoffing at someone else's ideas this time, and with good reason: they sucked. Dolly, which she had anticipated would be a bigger-budget version of the show of the same name that she hosted in Nashville in the 1970s, was compelled to air silly, embarrassing skits by network television executives. That previous performance had shown her innate talents for music, storytelling, and natural conversation with guests. However, ABC stipulated that each episode of her new show begin with her having a bubble bath on camera. In her book Dolly, she detailed her experience working with a room full of male writers and producers: "I was naive enough to think that what I wanted would somehow matter to the people in network television..." "Sometimes, I'd hear something mentioned and wait for everyone to laugh at how ridiculous it was, but the laugh never came." The joke was on me when the stupid concept was carried out."

When co-host Charlie Gibson asked Parton about her new show's low ratings on Good Morning America in 1987, she defended herself and her hopes for the show.

"We're just kind of weedin' out what ain't workin' really well, which is mostly things I didn't think would work to start with," Parton told Gibson at the time. "I think everyone is just trying a little too hard.... People are unsure what to make of it. 'Why are you taking a bubble bath on television?' I wondered. But, in any case, you do what you have to do."

"The hair may be false, but everything else is real, right?" replied dignified newsman Gibson.

Gibson never gave her a chance to promote her work in the segment. Instead of saying goodbye after he cued her departure, Parton named her forthcoming show's guests, including Patti LaBelle.

"Not to run through the whole cast or anything," Gibson grumbled. "Thanks very—"

"Well, I might as well—that's what I'm on television for," Parton said, her eyebrows arched in surprise. "You didn't think I got up just to say hello to you, did ya?"

"Absolutely, that's what I thought," Gibson replied with a similarly uncomfortable smile, and Parton talked over him again.

"I got up to advertise," she explained.

In the same year, in a rare instance in which a member of the press discussed Parton's wit rather than her body, Washington Post reporter

Jacqueline Trescott inserted another Parton interaction into a story about new-hire Gibson's flat presence next to Good Morning America co-host Joan Lunden.

"Some show business pros are quicker than he is," Trescott wrote. "When he asked Parton if she had tested the water slide at her Dollywood theme park, she answered, 'It's not the kind of ride for a woman with a haircut like mine.' Gibson moved on to her successful diet and inquired about her waistline measurement. 'Between the ages of 18 and 23,' Parton said. People believe I'm largely busted, but that's because I cram it all in.' He then inquired about her lucrative contract with ABC to produce a series of variety shows, to which she replied, 'It takes a lot of money to make a person appear this cheap.'

"Swallowing his comebacks, as the control room collapsed in convulsions, Gibson signed off, 'Thanks ever so much.'"

Parton also had the final laugh regarding her TV show. ABC had to pay her millions to cancel the show due to a well-negotiated contract. She also left with a deeper understanding of the corporate world, which she detailed in Dolly: My Life and Other Unfinished corporate, in a rare case of overriding her innate diplomacy and going for the throat. Don't trust the men in suits, she cautioned, and don't be concerned with their assessment of your worth.

"… "Despite the fact that the ratio is better than in some other industries, show business is still essentially a man's world," Parton wrote. "That can be difficult to deal with as a woman." Especially if you're a five-foot-two blonde with a southern drawl. Furthermore, with each cup size, the difficulty factor is multiplied by two."

Parton's professional answer to the challenge was to use it to her advantage.

"There are basically two kinds of men you have to deal with in business: the ones who want to screw you out of money, and the ones who want to screw you, period," she said. "I should state unequivocally that I am not interested in screwing anyone [professionally]." I never want more than what is just. The trouble is that I never desire anything less. In the old-boy business school, if a woman walks away from the table with what is rightly hers, the man feels screwed anyway. That, I must confess, adds to the satisfaction of getting a good deal. "How did it go for you, old boy?"

Parton was in full bloom as the 1980s faded, becoming the lady we know today: a clever business shark with a hyper-sexualized physical presence crafted for her own power and delight. By that time, what man's head did she need to turn? She was in her forties and had long been the boss.

Her music video for "Why'd You Come in Here Lookin' Like That," from her famous album White Limozeen, from 1989, is a corny but hilariously satirical staging of auditions for the male lead in a music video. She didn't create the number-one single, which laments how good a bad boy's a$$ looks in "painted-on jeans" and which she still performs with conviction at the age of seventy-one. But she's in charge of the film, watching from a dark theatre seat with the house lights turned off while men go on stage, flex their muscles, and play caricatures of various types of jerks. She chuckles and still likes them. ("I think they're all really sweet," she says to the casting director when he asks her opinion.) Her prize for Christian endurance: A finely sculpted janitor in cowboy boots and a cut-off denim shirt walks into the spotlight by mistake with a push broom. Perhaps in response to Charlie Gibson, Johnny Carson, Ronnie Milsap, and all the powerful, renowned men who neglected her artistry in favour of criticising her body, Parton stares the janitor in the eyes and says, "You're hired."

MEDIA SCRUTINY

When Dolly Parton visited the United Kingdom in 1983 for a television special called Dolly in London, a male reporter at a press conference questioned her if it was true that she did not consider herself a sex symbol. She claimed that she dressed in this manner not as a gimmick, but because she was "impressed with the people back home"—a reference to "trashy" ladies whose cosmetics and hair dye she had wanted in a rural region where few women had access to such things due to poverty and religious restrictions. She relished the picture she could now afford to paint.

"I'm feeling sexy," Parton admitted. "I enjoy being a woman. If I had been a male, I would have been a drag queen."

After a humorous reference to Best Little Whorehouse and bouts of laughing, a female journalist earnestly addressed Parton about sex work. The reporters in the room gasped, as if they sensed something accusing about the question or its timing. Parton's smile faded somewhat, and she took a moment to compose herself.

"Oh, I close the whorehouse," Parton laughed before becoming serious. "I adore everyone.... And, as I already stated, who am I to pass judgement? "I've got my own problems." Parton took a breather, but the room remained silent. She returned her attention to the questioner, as if to ensure that she, too, would have to squirm. "Are you a prostitute?" The woman bowed her head, embarrassed.

The old boys came in various forms for Parton: Hollywood directors, Nashville producers, and media interviewers. However, as demonstrated by the female journalist in the UK, Parton's interactions with women were frequently just as problematic.

On The Barbara Walters Special in 1977, Walters caught up with Parton at a rodeo in Kansas City, a gig her great popularity had not yet outgrown. Walters interviewed Parton, then thirty-one and just starting out in pop music, on the tour bus she shared with her band. Walters asked her if there was any "hanky panky" between Parton and her band; if she hit puberty at a young age; if her breasts were real; why she wore the tacky wigs and makeup; and how she could possibly keep a husband from straying if she was always on the road. (Parton: "I've got better things to do than to sit around in my room thinking', 'Oh, what's Carl doin' tonight?'")

Walters asked Parton to stand up at one point.

"I want people to see—you know," Walters remarked, her hands forming an hourglass.

"I'm not all that curvy in this outfit," Parton said as she rose to her feet.

"Oh, it's not bad," Walters remarked, looking over at the camera team to ensure the shot was good while Parton put her hands on her hips and endured the prank. "Do you give your measurements?"

"No," Parton replied. "I always just say I weigh a hundred and twenty."

Parton eventually felt forced to state that she was a human person.

"I'm very real where it counts... and that's inside—as far as my outlook on life and the way I care about people and the way I care about myself," Parton told the crowd. "Show business is a money making joke."

"But do you ever feel like a joke?" Walters asked, her tone more of a statement than a question. "That people make fun of you."

"Oh, I know they make fun of me," Parton confessed. "All these years, people [sic] thought the joke was on me, but it was on the public." I know what I'm doing and can change it at any time."

Parton went on to explain that her inner security—in her skill, in her good heart, in all the things Walters didn't question her about—was precisely why she could "piddle around" with makeup and clothes in a way that showed she was in command, not society and its would-be approbation.

The fact that the 1977 interview is distressing in retrospect demonstrates that women have gone a long way, at least in terms of media portrayal. While women are still subjected to sexist questions, most of today's major talk-show presenters would not treat Parton with such contempt, and if they did, an army of enraged Twitter users would be on their tail.

Even friendly interviewers like Oprah Winfrey, with whom Parton clearly shared mutual fondness and respect, were fascinated by Parton's figure. On her late-eighties talk show, Winfrey—no stranger to unrelenting attention over her body—had Parton get up twice for the audience to examine her.

Phil Donahue threw his hat into the sexist interview ring.

"I know guys who wouldn't let you out of the house," Donahue said to Parton on his hit talk program in the mid-eighties. Parton chuckled and assured him that her husband was not controlling. An audience member then inquired whether her husband had assisted her in her profession. Parton claimed that he prefers to stay out of her business issues and the trappings of show business.

"That's hard to believe he could be so removed from your professional life," Donahue said.

Parton responded thoughtfully, and then Donahue appeared on stage, holding out his hand to her. He'd stopped listening and moved on to—you guessed it—the next item.

"You won't mind if I just ask you to stand up for one second," Donahue replied, helping her to her feet.

Donahue and Winfrey both asked Parton about her lack of children. She was over forty at the time, and the topic had switched from "will you?" to "why didn't you?"

"That's by choice, isn't it?" Donahue inquired.

"No, actually, I can't have children," Parton said, repeating the spiel she told Winfrey about "female problems." Parton has admitted in recent years that the truth was more complicated; prior to her partial hysterectomy, she had considered having children but instead focused on her career—a preference so unacceptable for a woman of child-bearing age at the time that she circled around it when answering the question over the years.

These interview time capsules, which may reveal more about the cultural moment than the interviewers, amount to a comprehensive compendium of all the questions successful women—from celebrities to politicians to any woman with a profession in the public eye—are asked whereas men are not.

Socioeconomic class, on the other hand, has emerged in the American mind even later than race or gender. On her television special, Walters inquired about Parton's youth, to which she replied earnestly about the log home, the Little Pigeon River, and the many children. Walters then interrupted with a tone I'm familiar with: the upper-middle-class or rich lady dismissing the origins of a "poor" woman.

"Dolly, where I come from, would I have called you a hillbilly?"

Parton grinned. "If you had of, it would have been something very natural, but I would have probably kicked your shins or something." Walters did not laugh, while Parton did.

"But when I think of hillbillies, am I thinking of your kind of people?" Walters went on.

Parton had the opportunity to answer in real time on television and hoped that the producers would cut the tape fairly. Print was a far riskier proposition: speaking with a writer, usually a man, and then leaving him to write whatever he wished.

Chet Flippo, the longtime premier country music reporter, unfurls a middle-aged man's conquering fantasy about the time he spent with Parton for the story in one particularly barf-worthy Rolling Stone story from 1977. He imagines the encounter as a date, and she rides next to him in a convertible—he should have booked dinner reservations, he tells her. He made a point of mentioning that she had a few talks in her hotel room, which was usual procedure for celebrities conducting press on the road. He closed with a remark about Parton's newly emerging breasts as a child and the other kids pulling at her jacket to see what was below, and a reader wonders if he's just making stuff up. Magazine journalists were not known for taking precise notes at the time, and in this case, the gonzo male-writer adventure was at Parton's expense.

What do you do if you're Dolly Parton and you've been subjected to these ridiculous celebrity interviews for decades? You take a movie part that allows you to play a member of the media. Parton plays a small-town woman who leaves her deadbeat lover to start a new life in Chicago in the 1992 romantic comedy Straight Talk. She ends up as a radio talk-show "psychologist" who is compelled to hide her working-class origins and lack of a college degree.

In her book, Dolly Parton stated that she enjoyed making Straight Talk because director Barnet Kellman "was willing to share what he knew with me" and "had a nice way of doing it." Her inherent wit was allowed to shine through, with her own countryisms frequently making an appearance in the script, which finds her at odds with (and falling for) a cunning newspaper writer. Just as she had previously set a male employer straight in 9 to 5, regained the breast joke, and changed the name "Hollywood" to "Dollywood," she took control—and put herself in the interviewer's chair—with Straight Talk.

THE FREEDOM TO WORK

To have Steinem or someone representing her on social media appreciate a brief description of my mother—raised in abuse and poverty, seventeen when she became pregnant with me, tenacious as a bill-paying worker, intellectually and creatively gifted but unable to attend college, coveted as a woman deemed beautiful—completed my bifurcated socioeconomic experience.

That evening, at Steinem's address on the campus of the University of Texas, I was startled by her explanation for how such virulent misogyny could dominate the presidential election in 2016. According to Steinem, the moment a woman is statistically most likely to be murdered by her male abuser is when she flees. The terrible danger of losing control of her is what causes the violent ex-husband to snap.

Extending this concept to a patriarchy losing control of half of the US population would explain a lot of what has happened in recent years: The murder of abortion practitioner George Tiller in Wichita in 2009, Hillary Clinton's treatment and defeat in 2016, and the consistent track record of violence against and hate of women among male perpetrators of this century's mass-shooting epidemic. It might also explain how a self-assured, powerful woman like Dolly Parton became a boob joke.

Parton, like Steinem, is a symbol of twentieth-century American womanhood who is still going strong today, maybe with the vigour that other women her age who made more conventional decisions must contribute to their grandkids. Steinem did not come from a wealthy family, but the two ladies had very different socioeconomic experiences: one went to college, while the other took a guitar to Nashville. They both blazed the route for us to nominate a woman for president in 2016 in different ways and with distinct strategies.

When a woman becomes president, she will face the same sexist media questioning that women like Dolly Parton, Gloria Steinem, and Hillary Clinton have encountered, as well as criticism for her appearance and decisions. She will remember the times when males had power over her, whether it was the harassment Doralee endured for a job, the body-shaming Parton endured in Hollywood, or the second-guessing she faced from accountants on her own payroll. She will, however, be this country's first female CEO, and her leadership will undoubtedly be affected by the hardships of womanhood.

While their boss is chained and collared in his own bedroom in 9 to 5, the triumphant female employees rebuild the entire company with a flurry of overdue raises, recognition for cubicles full of women, and some productivity-enhancing remodelling.

To offer some females the possibility to similarly reconstruct this diseased democracy, we must give women the freedom to practise feminism however they see fit, whether we think it is correct or not. Women rejecting female supporters of Democratic socialist Bernie Sanders in the 2016 primaries is similar to Barbara Walters mocking Parton's fashion choices in 1977.

If Parton's difficulties and triumphs as an implicit rather than explicit feminist teach us anything, it's that the most true female power does not always correspond with a movement's ideology. If you take Parton's decisions from thirty years ago and compare them to what activists, academics, and other movement-approved experts said and wrote at the same time, I would gamble that Parton's feminism has aged just as well, if not better.

Fortunately for all of us, a new generation of female leaders has profited from both, whether directly or indirectly. They didn't all go to college, but they are all the daughters of 9 to 5—the children against whose life Parton's transformation from country star to corporate empress to worldwide icon can be traced. They are old enough to be divorced but young enough to be asked when they will have their first child; old enough to recall record players in every house but young enough to have been influenced by hip-hop. They witnessed their mothers being patronised and abused so that future generations would not have to, and they are prepared to reverse the achievements won by anti-feminist backlash over their lifetimes. Today, they are the three ladies who are fed up with the office and are ready to band together to hog-tie the male boss until they get some goddamn respect.

Some may see 9 to 5 as a revenge fantasy, but I see it as a fable about justice. It is not their boss's suffering that they seek, but rather their own equitable treatment—a desire that could only be interpreted as misandry in the perspective of male privilege.

During Parton's immensely successful 2016 tour in support of her album Pure and Simple, she provided a running commentary between song performances to ensure everyone knew who was writing the checks. "He's handsome, ain't he, girls?" she said of the hot masculine cowboy who brought out her instruments. Isn't he cute, boys?... "Make yourself useful and ornamental," as the ancient adage goes.

She told the audience that the fired drummer had scowled at her show clothes. It was meant to be a simple, stripped-down performance evoking a Tennessee front porch rather than a Vegas mega-show, and here was Dolly with her customary rhinestones, huge hair, and heels. He advised her to simplify her outfit as well.

Parton, who has become an expert at determining what the public learns, is meticulous with details. But this story—of a male employee giving Parton stage advice when she's been successfully directing her own music productions for decades—sounded accurate, and she clearly liked telling a narrative about being the boss.

She recalls times when she wasn't. She featured a black-and-white photo of Wagoner ceremoniously delivering a piece of valuable jewellery to her twenty-something self in her book Dolly; young Parton wears a beehive wig and a tight, obedient smile. The caption reads, "Me and Porter: Oh boy, a ring, but what I really wanted was a raise."

Parton didn't just receive a raise in the end; she got the entire world, and the drummer she hired for this tour evidently didn't hear. She told him the two words that every woman should be able to say: "You're fired."

"I abandoned him in Nashville." "I saved a lot of money," Parton added, fondly gesticulating toward the drum machine that took his position. "And it doesn't talk back."

CHAPTER 4

DOLLY PARTON CEMENTS HER ICON STATUS

Dolly Parton reunited with 9 to 5 co-stars Jane Fonda and Lily Tomlin to present an award at the 2017 Emmy Awards. Fonda and Tomlin were both nominated for Emmys for their roles in the Netflix comedy series Grace and Frankie, in which they play upper-class friends in Southern California, and Parton was nominated for producing the 2016 television movie Christmas of Many Colours, in which she plays an Appalachian sex worker.

Fonda emphasised Parton and Tomlin's roles as feminist elders onstage.

"Back in 1980, in [9 to 5], we refused to be controlled by a sexist, egotistical, lying, hypocritical bigot," Fonda was quoted as saying.

To applause, Tomlin said, "In 2017, we still refuse to be controlled by a sexist, hypocritical, lying, egotistical bigot."

Parton, for her part, joked about a season-two storyline from their show: "I'm just hoping that I'm going to get one of those Grace and Frankie vibrators in my swag bag tonight."

Hers was the least politically charged of the three. It was also the one most likely to irritate a man like Donald Trump, for whom women exist for his pleasure, lose value as they age, and require a man to attain sexual pleasure. What could be more anti-Trump than a wealthy 71-year-old woman fantasizing about a sex toy on public television after his name is mentioned?

The stars of that feminist film found themselves confronting the past in the present, their imaginary office boss elevated to the position of world leader.

Like the rest of the country, where conservatism now shapes the law and controls the White House, the country music industry is reversing the achievements gained by women in the late twentieth century. According to Forbes magazine, female musicians' songs accounted for fewer than 10% of country radio plays in the first half of 2016. Only five female musicians appeared on Billboard's Top 30 Country Airplay charts at the same period.

Keith Hill, an important country-radio consultant, explained why stations keep their rotations largely male the previous year. Hill told Country Aircheck, "If you want to make ratings in country radio, take females out." He described women as "just not the lettuce in our salad." Luke Bryan, Blake Shelton, Keith Urban, and other artists are the lettuce. Female tomatoes make up our salad."

The remark triggered a long-overdue debate about an old issue, and female artists were outraged. Martina McBride raised funds for her charity by selling "tomato" t-shirts. Jennifer Nettles described the situation as a "big old vagina-shaped opportunity."

Men and women in the music business defended Hill's remark with statistics and data: There aren't enough good female albums, female songs don't test as well, and when it comes down to it, female listeners prefer male singers. But this was not always the case. Whatever variables are driving such statistics, it says more about current societal attitudes than it does about the quality of women's music.

The last time Dolly Parton had a solo number-one song, "Why'd You Come in Here Lookin Like That" in 1989, female artists were riding high in the industry, paving the way for Reba, Faith, and Shania's halcyon 1990s. A recent Stanford University study, however, discovered that, despite record labels continuing to promote new female musicians, women have slid down the charts since the millennium's turn.

Parton has attributed her own absence from the charts to the fact that she has reached a certain age as an artist. "When the new country came along, any artist over the age of thirty-five was thought to be a has-been," she told Rolling Stone in 2003. "And, Lord, I've been around so long that people regard me as a legend." But I wasn't done yet. I felt like I was better than I had ever been before. I feel like I'm only now becoming experienced enough to know how to operate in this industry. 'Well, hell, I'm not going down with the rest of those old farts,' I thought. I'm going to try some new approaches.' And that is precisely what I did."

Parton established her own record company in 1994, at the age of forty-eight, when pop sounds dominated the country music market. "I thought, 'Well, now I can record the stuff I really want to,' and I don't have fourteen managers and record executives saying, 'Oh, you gotta be more commercial, you gotta be more pop,'" she said in an interview with Rolling Stone. "I told myself, 'I don't care if I write a six- or seven-minute song—I'm going to tell the story.'" I'm not going to say to myself, 'Oh, I'll have to trim this down to fit the radio.' Fine if they play it on the radio. They probably wouldn't, and they don't care anymore."

Whether they're underplayed on country radio or not, today's new female singer-songwriters who follow in Parton's footsteps—old twang, modern ideas, gothic country themes, spiritual vulnerability— get favourable reviews, sell records, and sell out performances. However, such performers, from Miranda Lambert to emerging revelation Kacey Musgraves to indie fave Valerie June, are working in an industry that is currently betting against them.

KEEPING IT REAL

Parton's late-career moves have demonstrated a preference for honesty over chart success. Parton has released almost a dozen solo albums of new songs since going rogue with her own label in the early 1990s. Some of it was released just as slick pop country singers like Keith Urban and Rascal Flatts were sweeping over the radio, including a Grammy-winning cover of Collective Soul's rock hit "Shine" in 2001.

The music from the earlier part of her career, on the other hand, has become her signature and is now being discovered by a generation born after Parton's disappearance from country radio. She appears to be a spiritual godmother to them, her big-haired 1970s picture on devotional candles in trendy stores and online shopping carts. A word a friend of mine recently used to describe a popular public radio broadcaster seems suitable to characterise Dolly's job today: "one of the few living astral moms."

Whether or not Parton has another blockbuster success, her entire existence is now recognized as breaking ground—for female artists, underprivileged girls with dreams, and women who want to be bosses without hiding their breasts. Parton's late awakening was slow, but the tipping moment may have been England's Glastonbury Festival in 2014.

After being without a manager for seventeen years, Parton engaged Nashville manager Danny Nozell to assist organise a tour in the early 2000s. Nozell devised a strategy for marketing her work to young people all around the world. She sold out a European tour in 2007, an arena tour in 2008, and two Australian tours in 2007. From 2006 to 2013, Parton turned down scheduling requests from Glastonbury, an enormous, undeniably rock-and-roll event. According to a 2014 interview with the Guardian, her ardent fan base has been global for decades, but she was concerned that the event wouldn't be a suitable fit.

When Parton eventually hit the stage as a Glastonbury headliner in 2014, she had no idea what was about to happen: An estimated 180,000 people attended her concert, making it the largest crowd in festival history, surpassing the numbers for a Rolling Stones performance. Another 2.6 million people tuned in live on the BBC, making it the network's largest-ever audience for festival coverage.

Glastonbury was a long way from Parton's childhood farm in East Tennessee, where she fashioned a tin can microphone and sang for the hogs. She had left that farm fifty years before, but she paid tribute to her roots for the enormous international audience with a song called "Mud," written for the infamously muddy festival. "I grew up on a farm," says Parton, "so this mud ain't nothin' new to me."

In recent years, Parton's effective method for connecting with new fans has included collaborations with much younger musicians. Parton sings a duet of her own number-one hit from 1980, "Old

Flames (Can't Hold a Candle to You)," which Kesha's mother, Pebe Sebert, composed, on Kesha's most recent album, released in August. Parton recorded Brandi Carlile's "The Story" earlier this year for an album benefiting a foundation that helps refugee children. She was nominated for a Grammy in 2017 for Best Country Duo/Group Performance for her "Jolene" album, which was reworked by the young a cappella group Pentatonix.

Parton has long supported her millennial goddaughter, Miley Cyrus, appearing on her Disney TV show, bringing her onstage, and performing with her on The Voice, maybe to the benefit of both. My journalist friend recently told me that he was watching the World Cup with Hugo Chávez in a pub in Venezuela when Chávez's daughter told him that she and her friend adored the "new Miley Cyrus song" about a woman named Jolene. They were astounded when he showed them a video of the Parton original on his phone.

Many of the new fans may not be able to name more than five Parton songs, but Parton's presence is so diverse that they will have lots of opportunities to learn more. Her songs have been covered by a diverse range of superstars, including Patti Smith and Kitty Wells. Some of her films, most notably 9 to 5 and Steel Magnolias, have become classics. Late-career Parton, on the other hand, is a charitable force and an auspiciously progressive voice in conservative circles.

According to the charity, her literacy project, Imagination Library, has sent more than 80 million books to over one million children worldwide.

Her vocal liberalism on gay and transgender rights, gender equality, and other issues has pushed country music to develop, while her open Christian faith and homespun vernacular have helped her bridge the gap between crossover fans and the poor, rural South.

The University of Tennessee sponsored a history course in the fall of 2017 that used Parton's life story to study Appalachia in the twentieth century, from child labour regulations to today's economic challenges. There is a rose named for her, as well as a film, the 2015 indie Seeking Dolly Parton. Parton is now to country music what

Oprah Winfrey is to the media: a natural genius who has transcended an industry to transform society just by being herself.

Women's advancement in country music was part of the shift she oversaw; Nashville is still entrenched in patriarchy, but it has come a long way since she arrived in the 1960s.

Perhaps because of her looks and persona, Parton was not treated with the gravitas long ago afforded to, say, Loretta Lynn, whose life was mined for the Oscar-winning biopic Coal Miner's Daughter and whose music sparked the admiration and collaboration of indie darling Jack White.

But, in the twenty-first century, with awakened youthful fans and more female representation in the media that shapes narratives about her, Parton's place in culture evolves from objectified female body to divine feminine—a sassy priestess in high heels.

GIVING BACK

Parton has stated that one of her greatest professional joys is her interaction with the children who receive free books in the mail each month from birth to age five through the Imagination Library, which she established in 1995. In 2013, she told PBS NewsHour that her children dubbed her "the book lady," oblivious to her popularity. This fall, Parton published her first children's album.

"Children have always responded to me because I have that cartoon-character look," Parton told Time magazine in 2009, when her own children's book, I Am a Rainbow, was launched. "I'm overexaggerated and my voice is small and my name is Dolly and I'm kind of like a Mother Goose character."

Her interest in reading stemmed from her father Lee's illiteracy. That familial history, which was the catalyst for Parton's remarkable rise from poverty, could explain why the first book each child in the program receives is The Little Engine That Could, with its lessons on hard work and perseverance that are classic Dolly. The narrative has been played live at Dollywood's Imagination Playhouse, where many of the program's selections are brought to life.

To check age eligibility, Imagination Library, which is commonly enabled by local libraries, does not require any income documents or other hoop-jumping—just a brief form with an address and the child's birth date. This move by the Dollywood Foundation demonstrates that someone involved understands what it's like to be a needy youngster. Because everyone is eligible, the most vulnerable children can benefit without feeling embarrassed about being recipients of a poor-people's program.

Parton's relief money for last year's Smoky Mountain wildfire victims were similarly devoid of red tape. Affected households, whether homeowners or renters, were requested to produce evidence of address in order to receive $1,000 each month for six months from the Dollywood Foundation. Parton made an announcement to some of the nine hundred families who had received aid at the end of that period, last May, and the Tennessean released footage of her encounter with one beneficiary.

"I'm going to give you an extra $5,000," Parton stated, bringing the total present to $11,000 for each home.

"An additional—" stated an older man wearing a University of Tennessee baseball cap.

"That's like a surprise bonus," Parton replied, smacking him on the back of the shoulder.

"God bless you for doing this for us," he said solemnly. "For all these people."

"It's the very least I can do," Parton explained. "I'm from the Smoky Mountains." This is, after all, home. "Doesn't charity begin at home?"

A white-haired woman seated next to the man spoke up. "Nobody but you would be so kind and generous," she began to cry. Standing, Parton wiped the woman's tears away.

"I'm sure nearly anybody up here would do that," Parton stated. "These are good people."

"You're our people," said the man, nodding. "Whether we're your people or not, you're our people."

"You're my people," Parton declared.

To address the long-term needs of individuals who lost their homes and other possessions, she donated $3 million to establish the Mountain Tough fund, which allows social workers to acquire medication for fire-related health problems, rides to work, and other services for low-income fire victims.

From the millions of books mailed to children to the millions of dollars raised for fire victims, from decades of high school scholarships to Tennessee high school seniors to the health care foundation she established in 1983 and named after the country doctor who delivered her, I've witnessed surprised reactions to Parton's philanthropy. One imagines that other renowned people are as generous as she is. But I've never seen anyone as caught aback by celebrity philanthropy as those who learn about Parton's.

Perhaps this is due to the fact that for the majority of her charitable contributions throughout the years, there has been no photo op or publicity release—just a quiet check and Parton's name on a board of directors. Parton's Imagination Library, in particular, maintained a low profile for nearly three decades, which must have been her preference at the time. But, in a 2009 documentary about the book program, children's author Robert Munsch got to the bottom of why her wonderful heart is such a revelation.

"I thought of Dolly Parton as this singer with the really big boobs who was in the movies with, like, the really big boobs," Munsch told me. "I didn't really have much of an idea."

HITS AND MISSES

Parton's career and empire are not without flaws, despite her thoughtfulness and self-awareness. Dixie Stampede, a dinner-theatre experience celebrating its 30th anniversary in 2018, is one truly troublesome rhinestone in Parton's corporate crown.

The daily entertainment, held in a 35,000-square-foot rodeo arena with seating for over a thousand people, incorporates horse-riding acrobatics such as barrel racing and musical shows as attendees eat chicken with their fingers. While Parton's theme is normally a class-conscious plea for love and inclusion, Dixie Stampede is a blatantly patriotic celebration laced with white-washed nostalgia for the Antebellum South. The show's primary topic is the Civil War, and audience members are asked to choose which side they would support.

Dollywood and her adjoining water park are located in Pigeon Forge, while a second one is in Branson, Missouri. Another was at Myrtle Beach, South Carolina, for eighteen years before Parton paid $11 million to transform it into a pirate-themed dinner-theatre attraction in 2010. In 2003, a facility near Disney World in Florida opened and closed five years later.

The remaining Tennessee and Missouri facilities received a $2.5 million makeover in 2015, which included new music and visual effects. By that moment, more than 20 million individuals had visited Parton's website.

Years before that update, I visited the Branson location with my family and found it to be far removed from Parton's spirit and physical presence. A tape of Parton's voice played from the speakers several times during the show, implying that she herself could come, which I found annoying and demeaning to the intelligence of the audience.

In terms of the event itself, I grew up going to rodeos and used to enjoy a good barrel racing just as much as the next gal. But I was in college when I waited in line at Dixie Stampede, learning about my home state of Kansas' critical role in triggering the Civil War by declaring itself a free state. During that time, considerable blood was shed near the border of slave-holding Missouri; Kansas maintains a difficult relationship with Missouri and Confederacy pride to this day. Perhaps this is why, even as a very uneducated and privileged young white woman, I was unimpressed with a plot that sanitised the Civil War as cheesy entertainment.

Following the refurbishment, Slate culture writer Aisha Harris wrote an overdue critique of Dixie Stampede, calling it a "lily-white kitsch extravaganza that play-acts the Civil War but never once mentions slavery." The Confederate flag does not appear to represent the South, but a grey banner suggests the hue of that army's outfit. The performance concludes with the message that we are all citizens of the United States of America.

Harris attended two 2017 performances to study her piece and was surprised by the number of persons of colour in the audience and among the employees. However, she thought the production to be a frightening, delusory spectacle.

"Standing in front of the box office were two young women who looked like the cast of The Beguiled, or Southern belles from Gone with the Wind, greeting patrons as they made their way into the building," Harris noted in an email. "Once inside and past the ticket scanners, you were compelled to pose for a group photo in one of several partitioned quarters against a green backdrop." Rather than immortalising this unwelcome reenactment in the form of a $30 souvenir, I declined to have my photo taken and ran past, attempting to fit in with the family in front of me."

Harris, a Parton admirer, noted that this awful piece of Parton's portfolio illustrated the denial that permits white people to defend Confederate monuments or consider white-supremacist marches and anti-racism protests as moral equals.

"Even though the South is built upon the foundation of slavery, a campy show produced by a well-meaning country superstar can make you believe it's not," he wrote.

A few weeks after her story aired, Harris reported for Slate that she had contacted Dixie Stampede for a reaction and had been assured via email that they would "evaluate" her piece.

While the original response could be considered as lacklustre, Harris kindly conveyed her hope for meaningful change in a Slate follow-up. "As an admirer of Parton's other work in movies and music," she wrote in an email, "and as someone who believes that it matters how honestly we tell our nation's history, it's nice to hear that my review might inspire the show's creators to reconsider its framing and presentation."

This disrespectful portrayal of a horrible history is especially disheartening in light of Parton's longstanding support for the LGBTQ community, women, and the poor. Her statement on everything else, from race to political affiliation, has remained a general message of love. Parton's late-career force and presence now intersect with a tumultuous civic period. What is she going to do with it?Parton alluded to the 2016 presidential election and race-related police shootings and riots onstage during her 2016 tour. She alluded to the country's combustible situation before delivering a touching selection of folk songs popular during the last time our culture was at such a boiling point—during the start of her career, in the turbulent 1960s.

She sang "If I Had a Hammer" and other counterculture classics while her unplugged musicians joined her with an upright bass, guitar, and tambourine, adorned in rhinestones and holding forth with the strong voice from her diaphragm that I've always preferred to the soft, girly voice she affects for some of her hits. Many in the audience sang along, some through tears.

NIP IT, TUCK IT, SUCK IT

Ageing celebrities may sometimes face a moral reckoning. Do their deeds and principles endure the test of time as civilization evolves? Bill Cosby's claimed serial rapesII went unnoticed in the misogynistic world of his youth, but they are now the stuff of career ruin. Meanwhile, public opinion on Jane Fonda's Vietnam War protests, for which she was reviled for decades, has softened as public opinion on the war has become more critical.

Physical ageing is another test in the maturity process for female stars. Parton is well-known for having had extensive plastic surgery and is open about it. She believes she must preserve her appearance and strives to convey energy. "I have done it and will do it again when something in my mirror doesn't look like it belongs to Dolly Parton," she claimed in her autobiography published in 1994. "I believe it is my responsibility to myself and my audience." My spirit is too wonderful and lively to be trapped in a decaying old body if it doesn't have to."

Pamela Fox, a country music expert, stated in a 1998 American Quarterly essay that Parton's destitute upbringing gave her a sense of detachment from her own body—previously used for farm tasks, now for fitting into a costume.

"Dolly Parton" becomes a separate, almost reified persona which her body actually develops, Fox wrote during the surgical reconstruction procedure. Parton recognizes that gender is performance: getting the perfect hair colour, conforming to an unachievable hourglass body type. But it's a performance she can pull off with remarkable success.... She trades the class-based objectification of her past for gender-based objectification in the present. "The Dolly character is a literal manifestation of her own personal 'dream.'"

In that context, a move that would make some feminists scoff turns out to be an honest win. "I always said, if I see something sagging, bagging, and dragging, I'm going to nip it, tuck it, and suck it," she told CBS in 2004. Whatever is required. I mean, I look at myself as if I were a show horse or a show dog.... I've always had attractive boobs. When I was younger, I had a lovely body, but when I shed all that weight, I had them pumped up and patched up. They simply stand there like brave little warriors. They're huge, they're expensive, and they're all mine now."

Parton's feeling of body sovereignty is a defiant gesture in a culture that has become so obsessed with her breasts that the first cloned mammal, a sheep made from a mammary-gland cell in 1996, was named after her.

Parton's reaction to double expectations concerning male and female bodies is to mock men's ageing rather than embrace her own. Parton related the known story of her song "Jolene" during a 2003 filming of CMT's Crossroads series with Melissa Etheridge—a pretty bank employee grabbed her husband's eye early in their marriage, and Parton's song implored her not to accept him.

"I look at him now," she quipped between songs, standing next to Etheridge, "[and] I think about hiding his Viagra and saying, 'Go get him.'"

Later in the set, the pair sang another song about jealousy, Etheridge's early-career rock ballad "Bring Me Some Water." Parton sung the words passionately, changing the verb "whispering" to something more wild: "Tell me how will I ever be the same / When I know that woman is somewhere screaming your name." Parton's tone went from tormented to authoritative as the song progressed, and with a stated aside, she suddenly manufactured a younger man for her own amusement. "Hey, little water boy," Parton remarked, her palm on her hip, unsmiling. "Bring the bucket around." Etheridge burst up laughing.

Parton's longtime friend and duet partner Kenny Rogers mentioned his own notably altered visage and how Parton has chastised him for it during a 2013 Good Morning America appearance next to her. "When [the media] got on that whole plastic surgery thing, that was a bit painful even though it was true," says Rogers. "Dolly used to say, 'Look, ol' Kenny's been to Jiffy Suck again.'"

Parton, who sat next to him, held his chin in her palm and scrutinised his face while he tried to draw away. "I think he's really grown into his face-lift now, don't you?" she asked, laughing. "He looks great."

The disparity in treatment of Parton's and Rogers' legacies is less amusing.

Parton has written thousands of songs, and her cultural impact has been so profound that the National Endowment for the Arts awarded her the National Medal of Arts in 2005, the country's highest accolade for contribution to creative disciplines. Rogers, on the other hand, rose to prominence by contributing his smooth voice to someone else's lyrics.

"I take great pride in not writing hits," Rogers told NPR in 2012, following the publishing of his memoirs, Luck or Something Like It. "I write on occasion, but I believe that great writers have a need to write, and I don't have that need." If someone sits me down and says, 'Hey, let's write a song about this,' I can write.

Many music icons did not write their own songs, and Rogers' career accomplishments are enormous. His career, however, profited from Parton's. According to Rogers, he was recording "Islands in the Stream" solo with mediocre results when producer Barry Gibb remarked that they needed Parton to "make it pop." The song is now one of the best-selling duets of all time and a cultural staple. Parton did not write the song, but her presence alongside him in the studio and onstage may have assured his legacy.

"There's no question it's kind of the crown to everything," he remarked on GMA. "To have done the song with her and have it be so well received around the world." "No matter where I go, they always ask for 'Islands in the Stream.' "

Despite this, Rogers, not Parton, was named the second recipient of the Willie Nelson Lifetime Achievement Award at the Country Music Awards (a year after Nelson himself won it in 2012).

The award was given to Johnny Cash posthumously the following year. Then, in 2015, when Parton became the first female and fourth performer to earn the honour, she was cut off just as she began her acceptance speech.

During the tribute, Parton's 9 to 5 co-star and friend Lily Tomlin spoke before Jennifer Nettles, Pentatonix, Reba McEntire, Kacey Musgraves, Carrie Underwood, and Martina McBride performed her hits. One minute into Parton's speech when she eventually reached the stage, producers cued her to end it.

"They wanted me to expedite it. "They said they were behind," she said to the audience. "But we're talking about a lifetime here." She finished with a wide smile at the two-minute mark, stating, "I had a big speech, but they won't let me give it." Sharon Stone then walked carefully across the stage and presented Best Male Artist to Chris Stapleton, who was visibly mortified. "If Dolly's still back there," he went on to say, "I'd give her my time." However, the show moved on.

Twitter users across the cultural and political spectrum reacted quickly.

"Really, #CMAawards50, you couldn't let the legendary @DollyParton speak for a lifetime of country music?" "No bueno," tweeted film critic Carla Renata.

"Who in the holy hell wouldn't let @DollyParton finish her speech for her lifetime achievement award?!?" said conservative commentator Meghan McCain.

Darienne Lake, a New York drag queen, tweeted, "My biggest devastation of the night, cutting @DollyParton's speech short." At the #CMAawards50, everyone should be fired. EVERYONE!"

Later in the evening, Entertainer of the Year Garth Brooks was given enough opportunity to speak. I'm not implying that there was some grand plan to cut Parton off and provide more time to male performers. However, as the radio programming consultant's "tomato" remark demonstrated, show business is a world of gender calculations. And that night at the CMAs, someone concluded, if only in a quick instant affected by culture and latent bias, that Parton's address was worth less than a sequence of moments starring men.

SO MUCH SUBSTANCE

A woman's voice, whether on the radio, onstage, or in a presidential campaign, will be recognized to a point. The amount of airtime will be reduced. The speech will be shortened. Someone will yell, "Lock her up."

Parton, who is undoubtedly one of the least contentious people in pop culture, appears to face no direct opposition. However, as a female leader, she has had to deal with the sexist onus of "likability." "As a Southern woman, how do you speak your mind and take care of business while remaining likeable?" Billboard asked her in 2014.

Parton didn't appear to be bothered by the situation. "I'm open and honest," she said. "I don't waste time." If something is going on, I just say it. When I'm angry, I'll say a few foul words just to prove my point. I've said before that I don't lose my anger as much as I use it. I don't do either unless absolutely necessary because I value peace and harmony, but if you step into my domain, I will call you on it. 'Oh, you simply seem so cheerful,' people say. That's Botox for you."

The glass ceiling that hampered long-term public servants Hillary Clinton's political battle against a morally bankrupt, inept man is the same one that forced Dolly Parton to answer more inquiries about her measurements than about her music over the years. The two women's paths diverged dramatically. But, at about the same age, they experienced an experience—breaking through, achieving equality that they would never have.

Who will thereafter follow in Parton's footsteps and reap the advantages of her hardships? While many young artists look up to Parton as an inspiration, who can actually fill her shoes?

VH1 speculated a few years ago that one such performer could be hip-hop superstar Nicki Minaj. Jade Davis, a media critic, elaborated on the hypothesis, citing Minaj's enormous hair and curves, as well as her economic acumen.

"They're also both musicians in lowbrow, male-dominated genres," wrote Davis in his essay. "They both accept being objects in the locations where they are permitted to exist... Parton affectionately refers to herself as 'backwoods Barbie.' Similarly, Minaj's most well-known stage [persona] is Harajuku Barbie.... Despite drawing inspiration from the most phoney women on the globe, they keep it more authentic than anyone else. They don't have to writhe around with lubricant on their bodies or stand in front of blazing

'FEMINIST' placards. They live, breathe, and execute what everyone else is attempting to convey: "I own myself."

Indeed, Parton helped pave the way for the kind of feminism seen in contemporary pop music: offering out T&A on your own terms, rejecting objectification by having a good time with it. And she did so without sounding like a liberal American. A caller to CNN in 2015 asked Parton if she considered herself a feminist.

"Oh, I'm a—I'm a female and I believe that everybody should definitely have their rights," she went on to say. "I don't care if you're black, white, straight, homosexual, a woman, a man, or anything else. Everyone who has something to offer should be able to provide it and be compensated for it, in my opinion. But, no, I don't consider myself a feminist in the way that some do, since I just believe that we all deserve to be treated with dignity."

If, like me, you speak the language of college-educated campaigners, her response may shatter your heart. But I also speak another language—poor country—and can attest that as an independent adolescent in small-town Kansas who believed women and men should be treated equally, I might have offered a similar response. Much of what is wrong with our country now is that we do not share a common set of definitions.

Parton's gift to young women is an example, not a statement, in the context of her native class. A hero should have both qualities. But, if I had to choose between the two, I'd go with the latter.

Today's female creators are inspired by Parton's pro-woman example. A teenage Dolly Parton fan realises she is adopted in the 2011 Canadian film The Year Dolly Parton Was My Mom, which is set in rural Winnipeg in the 1970s. The feminist messages in the story are self-aware.

Tara Johns, who wanted to incorporate Parton's music in the film, was able to get the script to her through a series of contacts just before Parton embarked on tour. According to Johns of the women's lifestyle website She Does the City, Parton reacted with a faxed letter expressing that she had spent the weekend reading the script and was overjoyed. For a modest amount, Parton granted her permission to utilise nine songs, four of which were recorded for the soundtrack by Canadian singers such as Nelly Furtado and the Wailin' Jennys.

"No Canadian film could afford to buy those publishing rights at the going rate," Johns was quoted as saying. Parton even did a narration for the movie. After hearing Parton on the radio, Johns had the concept for the film.

"I'd never really paid attention to Dolly Parton. Yes, the music, but not the woman. "Because there were no distractions, no flashy sequins or hair or boobs or whatever, it was just really easy to listen to the substance," Johns added. "She blazed a trail for so many artists who came after her, and I had no idea." That was a bit of a surprise. Under all of that, I thought it would be wonderful to know that Dolly Parton was a feminist when I was eleven or twelve."

Parton's trailblazing feminism, according to Johns, may have been unnoticed because of how she went about it. "The whole objectification that most women rail against, she took it, and she went to the wall with it," she added. "And in a way, it's a challenge, because she challenged the entire concept, the entire way of looking at women." Scrape away the very thin veneer of that objectified image, and you'll find a lot of substance.``

Parton's image experiments aren't always so deft. See her visit on The Queen Latifah Show in 2013, shortly after Latifah starred in the 2012 version of Steel Magnolias, which had an all-Black female ensemble, including Jill Scott, who played Dolly Parton's legendary beautician Truvy. Parton performed an original rap under a blond afro wig in apparent homage to Latifah, with whom she co-starred in the 2012 film musical Joyful Noise.

"Please welcome one of the baddest rappers in the game, straight out of 'ville," Latifah remarked to begin the section. "Nashville, that is."

While describing the story of her life, the song has a Grandmaster Flash-style sound and a traditional rap theme—don't attempt to step on this.

Parton began with a classic hip-hop crowd exchange—"Hey, hoooo, hey, hoooo"—before breaking into full East Tennessee: "I'm not calling' anybody names." I'm just saying hello!"

Parton then pointed out that while both she and Latifah had huge breasts, only one of them is known for working them. She motioned down at her chest while wearing a skin-tight black leotard with long sleeves (she is said to be tattooed).

"Look at dem go!" she rapped, referring to her breasts. "Hey, I'm tinkering. I'm at work. I'm twirling. Miley, I've got your wrecking' balls right now." Parton added a breath to the last syllable, a characteristic of the Southern Protestant accent. "She'll be comin' round the mountain when she comes,' ' she began to croon above the beat.

The performance, which could have been conceived by the producer, is unsettling to see. In encouraging Latifah to battle, she mentioned being a member of a "redneck mafia," presumably unaware that this may conjure up images of white supremacy in the South for some viewers. Parton's honest but clumsy purpose appears to have been to remind Latifah's audience that she, too, was anOther" of sorts, playing her way out of the role society had assigned her.

"You may be the queen," Parton declared, "but I am the white-trash princess." "Me and Honey Boo Boo." Parton's remark about a hit reality program about a child beauty pageant finalist and her "trailer trash" family was heartbreaking since she is well aware of the exploitation at work in such entertainment. She, like the little child, has been the subject of late-night talk-show jokes. But Honey Boo Boo had no option, and to some extent, neither did the family who was granted a much-needed check by the TLC network.

Hip-hop citing Parton is more successful than Parton mentioning hip-hop. Minaj, for example, twerks while daring you to insult her, calls out Parton's goddaughter Miley Cyrus for cultural appropriation, and makes sure her curves are in your face while doing so. She closes her rap verse on Drake's "Make Me Proud" with a direct invocation: "Double D up, hoes." "Dottie Parton."

GOD'S LITTLE DOLLY PARTON

Part of Parton's power as a woman stems from her ability to retain some of the little girl she once was, not just as the main character in a song about a coat stitched from rags, but also in her unwavering sense of wonder about the world.

Parton reveals a primitive delight for the natural world in one of the more stunning chapters of her book, Dolly: My Life and Other Unfinished Business.

"Sometimes I like to run naked in the moonlight and the wind, on the little trail behind our house, when the honeysuckle blooms," she wrote. "It's a feeling of freedom, so close to God and nature."

In other celebrity memoirs, this assertion could seem outlandish and doubtful, but Parton has just recounted what she previously knew as a child: the untamed liberty of the impoverished child whose parents are busy at work while she entertains herself. Parton's rural upbringing, as well as the talent that set her apart from other kids, meant that the Earth was her closest friend. It's easy to imagine a celebrity recognized for her groundedness recreating that experience on a walk through her Tennessee ranch.

"The full moon is my best time," Parton said. "It feels good to be without makeup, wigs, or high heels, just my little stubby self." "It's just God's little Dolly Parton all over again."

This is the spirituality—erotic, embodied, and free of man or dogma—that has been with Parton since her early days, coexisting with her Christian religion. Dolly identified three loves that shaped her the most: God, music, and sex. They are all visible in her rural East Tennessee upbringing: her pastor grandfather's severe Pentecostal faith, the homemade instruments she performed barefoot on porches, and the twelve children her mother bore probably due to a lack of birth control and a necessity for farm help.

Parton has refashioned and sewed these ideas together to create her own true existence, just like her inventive mother did with a box of rags. While pursuing a music career, Parton asserted sexual power—not just in connection to a lover, but to the entire world—and carried herself with a religion that manifests itself through Christianity yet finds its power within rather than beyond. ("The magic is inside you," Parton once said. "There ain't no crystal ball.")

Parton mused in her memoirs about starting a line of high-quality bras for large-chested ladies since she adored lingerie but found it lacking in her size. Her next thought is a lovely kiss-off to the pastor grandfather who chastised her as a prostitute when she was a teenager for wearing makeup and tight clothes. "Grandpa Jake is in heaven right now," she wrote. "I hope he's getting a kick out of seeing me go into business hawking the very things he used to chastise me for."

Parton has effectively forced the public to reckon with what patriarchy seeks to conceal by telling her life narrative through interviews, live concerts, books, and autobiographical TV movies.

Clarissa Pinkola Estés unearthed an archetype she said had been purposefully purged from myths, religious traditions, and culture in her important 1992 feminist book Women Who Run with the Wolves: Myths and traditions of the Wild Woman Archetype.

"This is how many women's teaching tales about sex, love, money, marriage, birthing, death, and transformation were lost," Estés writes in her book. "… Most old collections of fairy tales and mythos existent today have been scoured clean of the scatological, the sexual, the perverse (as in warnings against), the pre-Christian, the feminine, the Goddesses, the initiatory, the medicines for various psychological malaises, and the directions for spiritual raptures."

The "Wild Woman," Estés wrote, can be rediscovered via new stories, art, and community.

"I was fortunate as a child to be surrounded by folks from many of the ancient European countries and Mexico.... They, along with many others—Native Americans, Appalachians, Asian immigrants, and numerous African-American families from the South—came to farm, pick, labour in ash pits and steel mills, breweries, and domestic occupations. Most were not academically educated, yet they were extremely wise. They were the keepers of a priceless and nearly pristine oral legacy."

The exclusion of women from country radio by male executives is reminiscent of the exclusion of female stories from foundational and historical books. Parton's songs, life, and career demonstrate that neither can prevent a woman from being heard. She is a modern-day symbol of the rebellious woman, the Wild Woman of myth and feminist literature.

During the 1989 Country Music Awards, that woman was in her prime. Parton played Don Francisco's gospel ballad "He's Alive," which she covered on that year's White Limozeen album after being affected by it on her tour bus one night. A tight white robe wrapped her from neck to wrist to foot while she performed alone onstage at the CMAs. Her blond wig and gleaming red lips were everything but modest.

The song depicts the account of Jesus' resurrection through the eyes of Peter, who initially doubts the female apostle Mary Magdalene, who was the first person to see Jesus alive after his tomb was discovered empty. He and John discover the tomb empty, just as Mary had predicted, but fear his body has been removed by officials.

Parton sang the story at the CMAs with apprehension in her voice and on her face, her head cocked and eyes hazy, as if she was channelling the music from somewhere else. According to the Bible story, Peter eventually sees the risen Jesus with his own eyes and is overcome with a sensation of peace, joy, and relief. A bridge then shifted the song's key.

Parton expressed her realisation by turning toward the back of the stage and raising her arms. A stage-widescreen behind her was supposed to rise while she did so. However, there appeared to be a technological glitch, and Parton returned to the microphone to begin the triumphant breakthrough verse with her clear, booming pipes: "He's alive!" As she did so, the screen eventually appeared, exposing a great choir in angelic robes resounding "He's alive" higher on the scale.

I haven't practised Christianity in many years, but watching the old performance online gave me goosebumps and nearly brought me to tears—not because of the religion, but because of the transcendent accomplishment of the song, the voices, and the woman at the front of the stage in complete command, possessed by her own performance.

As the camera pans to the audience, at least one older man can be seen sobbing.

Parton appeared to grasp what had just transpired for a brief period. Her eyes grew clear and focused on the throng, and she smiled contentedly, as if to say, "Welp, we just brought this bitch down." She swaggered backward with a swing in her hips before thanking the choir. She had just completed her professional mission: to see God in a song while also allowing the rest of the world to see her.

DON'T NEED NO COMPANY

When Dolly Parton's long standing closest friend, Judy, got out of the Air Force early in her career, the two went to New York to party with Parton's new money from The Porter Wagoner Show. According to her autobiography Dolly, she was a country TV celebrity who went virtually unnoticed in New York City. They dressed up in short skirts and thick makeup and headed out on the town, each carrying a.38-caliber revolver in her purse. "I felt comfortable enough around a gun, and at that time I thought carrying one was the thing to do," Parton stated in an email.

Around 1970, New York was a grittier town, and they were twenty-something country ladies with a mission: to be evil. They went to a filthy movie theatre and sat down to see a pornographic film. This attempt at a harmless controversy, however, was unsettling—two young women in a bad-smelling theatre with a handful of men who were "the raincoat type." They were troubled by the film itself. "What we thought would be exciting and sexy was gross, filthy, and insulting," Parton wrote in an email. She and Judy exited.

According to the book, they slumped against a wall a few blocks down the street—"dressed the way we were"—to compose themselves. An inebriated man approached Parton and inquired about her rate as a prostitute. She told him to go find himself. "We don't need no company," Parton recalled.

He assaulted her in reaction, "grabbing at me in places I reserve for grabbers of my own choosing" and telling her she liked it. Parton took her Smith & Wesson from her purse and walked away. "I could hear him calling me a bitch as he walked away," she said.

Parton is as big a star in New York and around the world as she is in Nashville, and her entourage is armed. The parable, on the other hand, lives on. "Am I asking for it?" She has pushed society ever since with her powerful demeanour and daring appearance.

Parton released early on that people would perceive her as a cheap lady whose looks and sexuality demanded more instant attention than her work. Her mother used to say to her onstage, "I hope you get a blessing out of it." That's exactly what Patron did with the difficult assignment she was given by society.

As a result, she is a woman of contradictions: Someone who is "trashy" but has more class than the majority. Someone who dresses "like a hooker" and is a self-proclaimed homebody with a family. A chirpy blonde who is wiser than her male coworkers. A little girl who "escaped" by singing about the place she left. A Christian who behaves like a true Christian. A woman of great depth who was born and named after a toy doll—a phrase of endearment that also implies an unnatural thing made for the delight of others.

"If I have any charm, it's that I appear totally phoney, but I am completely real," Parton told Cineaste in 1990. "That's my magic."

She is a rare breed of icon, being both a sexual icon like Marilyn Monroe and a creative genius like Loretta Lynn, as well as a humanitarian force like Oprah Winfrey. Meanwhile, Parton entertains herself, and if she is a whore, she is equally the pimp who is turning herself out and the john who is enjoying it.

"You spent good money on me," Parton addressed the audience during one of her 2016 arena performances, as if she recalled how difficult it was to save up for a night out. How could she have forgotten? Half of the songs she sang had that topic.

Her memories of hard times were well received by the audience, as they always are. The most applause, however, came when she inquired if she should run for president.

We're unlikely to see a presidential bust of Parton, but her hometown of Sevier County did place a life-sized bronze statue of Dolly outside its downtown courthouse in 1987. She is a young woman with her hair pulled back, seated on a rock with an acoustic guitar, her jeans cuffed at the ankles to reveal bare feet in this representation. This Dolly Parton is more like the one who runs through the woods than the one who performs in arenas in rhinestone-covered jumpsuits.

"After my father died, one of my brothers told me that Daddy used to put a big oil drum full of soapy water and a broom in the back of his truck," Parton said on Jimmy Kimmel Live! in 2016. "And late at night he'd go down to the statue and scrub all the pigeon poop off."

Whatever kind of icon she is, whatever she represents to her fans and the rest of society—a wax sculpture wearing sequined shoulder pads in a Los Angeles museum of celebrity likenesses, a barefoot bronze in East Tennessee, or a living national treasure who defies easy categories—Parton survived and even changed a man's world so brilliantly that one occasionally sees an unlikely reference to perhaps the most powerful, least political feminist in history on T-shirts or online memes. Parton remembered on Kimmel that her father had a bumper sticker on his pickup that said, "Dolly Parton for President."

Printed in Great Britain
by Amazon